Leave Your Phone at the Door

Leave Your Phone at the Door

The Joy of OFFLINE

Howard Lewis

Radius Book Group
New York

Radius Book Group
A division of Diversion Publishing Corp.
www.radiusbookgroup.com

For more information, email info@radiusbookgroup.com

The publisher does not have any control over and does not assume any responsibility for author or third-party websites or their content.

First Radius Book Group Edition: March 2025
Hardcover ISBN: 978-1-63576-939-5
e-ISBN: 978-1-63576-941-8

Book design by Scribe Inc.
Cover design by Zoe Spurgeon and Scott Richmond
Interior art by Liam Walsh
Jacket design by Jen Huppert

Printed in the United States of America
10 9 8 7 6 5 4 3 2 1

Contents

Introduction

I am reminded with every passing day that I know a little about a few things and not much about the rest. Yet this blissful state of ignorance has contributed to my life in the most positive fashion, as it has always encouraged an innate sense of wonder and curiosity about the world around me. Take nature programmes. Whereas many people binge on costume dramas or gritty detective series, I am enthralled instead by the construction of termite mounds or the mating habits of the porcupine or the astonishing versatility of fungi. The evolution of planet Earth and its inhabitants represents a series of deeply intertwined journeys over millennia so my fascination also extends to human nature. And we are a peculiar bunch in our own way, whichever direction you care to look, all shapes and sizes, replete with our own strange sounds, bizarre appearances and odd rituals. But *Homo sapiens*, stepping gingerly out from the Miocene era, received the most extraordinary bounty of all—a far more sophisticated brain and the consequent gift of speech.

Other species have developed remarkable adaptations that enable them to communicate in a manner quite beyond our understanding but none of them can actually talk. Have you ever heard a pig reciting Latin verse or a monitor lizard reading out safety instructions? I believe not. Speech is a uniquely human attribute, wired into our very DNA, but the increasing use of technology has unwittingly subcontracted our real voice to third parties. Personal technology fertilises distance as much as proximity by removing the physical dimension and each time we use online tools another sliver of our humanity slips through our fingers. Life was far simpler in the Miocene. There was no app to advise the location of the most abundant hunting grounds nor fashion tips on how to best wear your freshly skinned bear pelt. You relied upon instinct, luck, experience and plain common sense for all your life skills. And perhaps a well-appointed cave in which to woo your beloved.

The creation of the OFFLINE concept was partly motivated by my realisation that many of these basic life skills only make a cameo appearance in our coddled and overweened new century. The excessive use of technology has dulled our minds and our senses. An awareness of the land and soil beneath our feet would represent a decent start. It is instructive to note the emergence of the digital detox retreat as a simple means for individuals to engage with nature, detach themselves from any media sources and properly appreciate the value of peace and quiet. But why is it so difficult to switch off voluntarily? What is so gripping about yet another newsfeed or banality on social media? Very little from where I am standing but there is an apparent desperation to keep up with events and to be perceived as being at the top of your game. It is a self-imposed addiction to attention and relevance and meaning that advertises both weakness and self-obsession.

Community in its truest form is an organic, living thing but the rise of the smartphone seems to have atrophied the ability of humans to communicate in a regular way. The experts say it is caused by the dopamine effect whereby nominally sensible people gorge themselves on the delusion that almost every online exchange will be satisfying, soothing or malleable in some measure and, therefore, a justifiable use of their time. A potent cocktail of hormones and neurotransmitters influences our cognitive powers so a quick hit of dopamine brings a quick reward. The unaffected modesty of the dumb phone that so many parents advocate for their kids today is a progressive move, if only to help their progeny to reclaim some of their childhood. The ability to send a text message or make a phone call is undeniably a good thing in both directions although the inference that a smartphone is an essential piece of kit for a young person is sadly indicative of lazy teaching, lazy parenting and lazy governance.

All stakeholders provoking initiatives to minimise smartphone usage face the triple obstacle of corporate greed, regulatory timidity and human nature itself. The first two are easily rectified if there is a will to change, although all the evidence suggests not. Human nature is a bit more complicated as the diminution of physical engagement means that the signals and nuances that historically shaped our conduct are no longer so prevalent. Babies learn how to interact by watching and mimicking their elders. Nobody gives them an instructional video to work it out for themselves. Adults are often even needier as they worry so much about their deficiencies and what they may do wrong they don't interact at all if it may expose them to potential criticism or mockery. And so a smartphone enables them to ring-fence their weaknesses and insecurities from prying eyes and frequently do so anonymously.

Our ancestors may well have squirrelled away a moose or two to survive the deep freeze but long-term planning and risk management models did not loom large on the agenda. Or at least no larger than the vast bulk of the woolly mammoth they sought to capture. Bellowing at them with its fearsome tusks at the ready, it would have required outstanding communication skills and teamwork on their part to bring it down. These early civilisations were by no means as primitive as you might imagine and two of their greatest inventions, fire and the wheel, are ubiquitous features of our lives today. These are not isolated examples. Consider the scale and imagination of the pyramids at Giza, built around 4,500 years ago without the benefit of any industrial mechanisation but with plenty of blood, sweat and tears. I suspect the health and safety executive did not possess much leverage there! Or the vision, innovation and sheer effort that brought to fruition the Hanging Gardens of Babylon, a mere 2,500 years ago. Nor should one overlook the complex of temples at Angkor Wat in Cambodia or the Inca citadel of Machu Picchu in Peru, the latter constructed in the foothills of the Andes no less. The past all too often provides us with a roadmap for the future if only we remember where to look.

All these prodigious accomplishments could only have been achieved by the use of verbal and visual cues alongside the heavy lifting. Whether you communicated quizzically, directly, forcefully, subtly, quietly, dramatically or collectively, whatever your mood or disposition, you spoke face to face. Unless you glowered or laughed or sighed in which case your thoughts or feelings required little embellishment. The economic impact of automation is not in doubt but its social impact is rather more questionable. Any activity that reinforces separateness presupposes that people are equipped to handle the vacuum into which they are transplanted and assume greater personal responsibility. But scope for experimentation and independent thinking sits uneasily when you have long been enveloped by the reassurance and tacit approval of a large organisation.

If you take a dozen people, whether Russians and Ukrainians or Israelis and Palestinians, you will find they broadly agree on eight issues out of ten. A home of their own, the means to support their families, access to education, security, healthcare, infrastructure, equal opportunities and the prospect of a fairer, more balanced society are all reasonable expectations. But the small potatoes of politics and religion are all too often allowed to infringe on these aspirations and it is a matter of much regret that both of them are given far more weight than they deserve through social media and related channels. The ability to talk in person is precious yet far too often words expressed online dominate popular opinion and are characterised by craven foolishness and grandstanding. The subtleties of tone of voice and body language, perhaps even mode of dress, may be either misinterpreted or lost altogether.

We live in an imperfect world. There is a pervasive but misguided belief today that technology and artificial excellence are an indisputable force for good. It has infiltrated almost everywhere. Sport is a glaring example of this downward trend. Historically, before the dawn of the action replay and its fancy successors, sport was as much a tale of knock-ons, dubious lbw decisions or line calls, sly conduct by players, egregious officials, miscarriages of justice and outrageous fortune or misfortune. All these ingredients are a metaphor for life itself. The element of jeopardy is being squeezed out by a craving in society for certainty but I much prefer a twinge of uncertainty which, of course, cuts both ways!

I possess no professional qualifications nor any academic credentials. I have never read a case study, let alone written one, never chaired a focus group and bring no defined expertise to the table. But a fair chunk of my life has been absorbed by observing, reading, challenging, head-scratching and asking plenty of questions, occasionally of myself. The human condition is endlessly multifarious and fluid but it can also become wedded to belief systems and behavioural patterns, regardless of any change in circumstances. The distinguished economist and author John Maynard Keynes famously stated that when the facts changed, he changed his mind. Quite right too! This is not a very radical notion yet there is a profound reluctance among the majority to deviate from accepted practice, unless there is a compelling or urgent reason to do so. Obviously, some things are immutable and never change so naturally you support your football club for life, recognise that Holbein, Rubens and Turner were artistic geniuses for the ages and, heaven forfend, never spread cream before jam on your scones!

This book is a loose medley of stories, anecdotes, experiences and observations which gestated upstairs for many years. Should it appear slightly uneven and haphazard on occasion, it will be entirely in character. The OFFLINE concept wriggled free from its chrysalis without any clue about its flight path. All I knew was that it was airborne and from that vantage point I witnessed the vagaries of society beneath me. Most graphic of all were the clusters congregating with those who looked or sounded similar to themselves and remained fearful and suspicious about even tiptoeing beyond their comfort zone. Conversely, OFFLINE threw caution to the winds and ignored all common convention, since at its core it is a celebration of the much underrated virtues of randomness and serendipity. Drawing together thirty or so disparate individuals from across the spectrum was an invitation to all participants to take a soft risk. And how eagerly they embraced it! I always aimed to assemble a motley crew so it variously encompassed doctors, dentists and deep-sea divers, politicians and mechanics, opera singers and philosophers, designers and bankers, students and retirees, museum curators and environmentalists, the whole shebang. I might even have invited Mr and Mrs Miocene if they were around although you will understand I could not vouch for their table manners. At each dinner, I would mix them all up, give them a vigorous shake and voilà! A concoction none of them had consumed before and all the more delicious for it. The OFFLINE mantra of wandering off the beaten track meant that numerous attendees trod some unexpected paths to their mutual benefit, especially the younger generation who were also startled to learn they had survived three hours unscathed without even thinking about their mobile device!

When did you last attend a block party for everyone on your street? The setting would be both familiar and unfamiliar, maybe a little raucous and rumbustious, but it would typically be a warm and shared experience nonetheless. There is a pressing need to reclaim our physicality, tactility and sense of freedom, each of which has dwindled in the modern era. The creeping invasion of corporate and governmental oversight into our lives has regulated our natural spontaneity but in a private capacity this has also spilled over into self-censorship. People all too readily discard one another from online groups if they do not meet the right criteria or question the manner or authority of the leading voices within. Exclusivity can offer some value but I much prefer inclusivity as it is multilayered. In the simple act of asking, you invite people inside your tent, cave, block party or whatever. Some may only participate on the fringe and some not at all but what matters most is that they feel valued and a part of it.

The coronavirus outbreak intensified existing mental and emotional vulnerabilities for a significant number of people. The desire for comfort and belonging was very evident, as everyday lives became compartmentalised due to public health strictures. However, one retrograde consequence thereafter has been the presumption that any face-to-face commercial transaction, whether in a coffee shop, bar, taxi or convenience store, can only be conducted by the use of a bank card or mobile phone rather than cash. Since when did money become quite so dirty? Yet this behaviour is just the tip of the iceberg, one more symptom of an automated world that reinforces a sense of physical distance so OFFLINE always sought to accentuate the reverse. It was as if the guests were all six years old again and I had given them the run of the candy store. The dinner proved an enduring and successful formula over some fifteen years precisely because I imposed so few rules and expectations upon them. All I asked was that they attended with an open mind and a generosity of spirit. I found that this laissez-faire approach brought out the best in people as, aside from sharing a few stories over the course of the evening, I allowed the room to find its own rhythm. But that rhythm was to be dramatically destabilised by events almost five years ago quite beyond my control and offered an apt reminder, if ever one needed reminding, that you never know for sure what may lie around the corner and that life is truly for living!

In February 2020, I flew to America for a trip that covered six cities in fourteen days. It was barely a month before coronavirus formally introduced itself to the world at large so all appeared relatively calm on the surface. Yet a rude awakening lay just around the corner. Indeed, when I travelled a fortnight later to Amsterdam, I witnessed masks and social distancing for the first time and realised that coronavirus was no longer a mere footnote in the newspaper nor an exclusively Asian phenomenon. It escalated for me only a few days later when an OFFLINE dinner I was hosting in mid-March was cast in serious jeopardy. One of the attendees was an Italian friend who was coming with his doctor wife. He revealed that she had spoken to former colleagues in Milan whose hospitals were becoming increasingly stretched by a highly infectious and insidious virus. The authorities had been overwhelmed by the speed with which the virus was being transmitted and were struggling to find even temporary solutions. Based upon her first hand information, he stated that regrettably they would have to decline the invitation and the following days brought more withdrawals from concerned attendees. I knew in all conscience I would have to defer the dinner until people regained the confidence to engage in conversation in a public setting. Little did I appreciate that it would be over two years before I hosted another OFFLINE dinner.

Part One
The OFFLINE Ethos

The Anatomy of OFFLINE

The essence of OFFLINE is twofold. On the one hand, it is simply the antithesis of online. Not that online is all bad. On the contrary, online is rather good, but what is not good at all is this latter-day obsession with it, whereby all those skills you learned at your mother's knee, like reading and writing and talking, are becoming dying arts. Yet the curious thing is that humans are social animals by nature and that physical interaction is a fundamental part of our being.

But there is another dimension to OFFLINE that is arguably even more important. Most people follow a fairly conventional path through life for good and sensible reasons—commercial exigencies, the demands of parenthood, all the usual suspects play their part—but what typically occurs is that they fall into a sort of comfort zone, an area densely populated by straightforwardness, by convenience, by familiarity and, I dare say, by a hint of laziness.

As a result, I believe it is very valuable and, indeed, very necessary, as you pursue that straight path through life, that you periodically veer OFFLINE. You can veer back on that path, of course, but sometimes that deviation of mind, body or soul can yield some surprising consequences and their manifestations might just challenge your view of the world.

We all communicated perfectly well face to face for thousands of years before digital media showed up, and, although personal technology certainly has its merits, it is not so transformational that we cease communicating face to face. Yet a significant swathe of the population struggles with the very notion of direct contact and its consequences. There is an overriding fear about what might go wrong in such interactions and this suspicion and negativity pervades other aspects of our lives.

The OFFLINE ethos is far more concerned with what may go right and acknowledges that the endless pursuit of perfection and excellence can be potentially destructive. I hope this book will help people maximise their personal worth in both a business and a social context, for the ability to develop empathy and rapport will become critical in a world dominated by algorithms and AI. The irony of social media is that it is profoundly antisocial, and the OFFLINE philosophy should enable those strangled by its grip to successfully reengage with real people in real time and real life.

One day a week, walk on the opposite side of the street to the station. You will still arrive at the same destination, but en route, you may notice the different facades of buildings, the sweep of the curve, kids on the way to school and dogs on the way to walk. This exercise reaffirms the duality of OFFLINE, which is less a shrine to the analogue world and more an invitation to celebrate the much underrated virtues of randomness and serendipity.

When Fate Lends a Hand

The genesis of OFFLINE began a long time ago. I was always a very curious boy, fascinated by people and places, books and ephemera. Once I hit adulthood, I metamorphosed into something of a newspaper and magazine junkie, variously hoovering up the mainstream press, international press, specialist press and underground press. Not much was off limits to me. I would often tear out articles to read later or in more depth, and, as I sifted through the pile, I would ruminate to myself that Tom would enjoy this one while Jennifer might like that.

So I grew into the habit of dispersing articles in a suitably indiscriminate OFFLINE fashion. It was simply a way of saying, "Hello, I was thinking about you." No more, no less. You might receive three in a week and not hear from me for three months, but the articles broadly fell into the following categories:

articles that I particularly enjoyed,

articles that I felt others would particularly enjoy,

articles that I felt were interesting or well written that others
should read anyway.

Nobody ever said to me, "What is this crap? Stop wasting my time!" On the contrary, the feedback was almost universally positive. One person, for example, would tell me that an article I had sent led him to pursue a successful business deal, another passed an article to his wife that she very much appreciated, while a third discovered a delightful but hitherto unknown hotel. It became evident to me that the majority of people possessed a real appetite for information, knowledge and insight but had neither the time nor the inclination to distil the vast profusion of material out there.

One day, I met a friend for a coffee and passed him another sheaf of articles to read. He was aware that I shared articles with others and wondered out loud what everyone else was receiving. That struck a chord with me, so I decided to bring a bunch of like-minded individuals together one evening for supper, either past recipients or those kindly disposed to the idea, to share a few more articles with them and see where the conversation took us. I booked a private room at The Bleeding Heart in Hatton Garden, historic centre of the London diamond trade, and gathered about twenty people. After my initial preamble about the OFFLINE philosophy, I asked them all to think back to their very first social engagement but they sat there rather puzzled, as if I had posed some kind of trick question.

So I got down on my haunches to give them a clue, patting the air no more than a foot or two from the ground. They looked even more puzzled so I got straight to the point. The first social engagement any of them had attended was a birthday party. Patting the air knee high symbolised the fact that we were all little people once upon a time. And what did they remember most fondly about the occasion? It certainly wasn't the food or their fellow guests or, indeed, the games they might have played. The one thing that either topped off a wonderful afternoon or salvaged them from an abyss of despair was the GHP—the going-home present.

I then declared that I had GHPs for the assembled, but, as they were all rather older and nobody's mother was waiting patiently outside, they would receive them at the start of proceedings rather than the end. Tottering around the room with a fat stack of envelopes, I called out their names alphabetically. "Where is Abigail? I have a present for you." Her hand shot up, and I gave her an envelope. She opened it and noticed half a dozen articles. Her neighbours on either side of her were curious about its contents too, as was the rest of her table, but I did not linger. "Ben? Where are you?" His hand shot up, and I repeated the same process. I was off again. "Chantal?" She flagged me down soon enough. And on it went until everybody had an envelope.

I rarely read the articles beforehand myself. I may have skimmed through them, but I am rather like a chef who tastes everything but eats virtually nothing! Each envelope contained three articles for every-one, but the balance resembled a potpourri. An article might go to perhaps half a dozen random individuals, or, on occasion, it might go only to one recipient, especially if it featured a theme that I knew they were personally interested in, such as space travel, Russian lit-erature, tennis or whatever. And I watched the action unfold before my eyes. Some participants were so consumed by the articles that they were oblivious to the rest of the room, while others were much more engaged by the selection elsewhere. Why do three people at my table have that piece on urban renewal, while I have a review about the conservation of giraffes? I have no idea!

Dinner was served shortly afterwards, so articles and envelopes disappeared from immediate view. It proved to be a swinging evening and many attendees wrote to me afterwards to express their pleasure at its mood and disposition and, indeed, the variety of guests. One stated he had a marvellous time and had read every article in his bun-dle once he was home, while another had equally enjoyed the occa-sion but confessed that he put his envelope under his chair when dinner arrived and forgot all about it. I was unfazed. The dispersal of articles was merely designed to pique their curiosity and create con-versation pieces. They could have used them thereafter to build paper aeroplanes for all I cared.

I vividly recall sitting back later in the evening, observing the dynamic across the room as a shock of positive energy. It was all about the physical interaction as people completely ignored their natural sense of caution and restraint, pointing, waving, drinking, arguing, eating, laughing, flirting or perhaps just sharing or swapping articles. And I thought to myself, "I can go home now. My job is done." But I stayed, of course, as so many pleasures were yet to emerge, and I recognised how embracing the virtues of randomness and serendipity had such a galvanising effect. I realised too that I had accidentally devised a formula that I could replicate in myriad ways.

The concept certainly offered plenty of scope for experimen-tation. One gathering drew about seventy-five guests as a sort of extended cocktail party, but, although the room hummed and purred in all directions, I felt something was missing. It did not encourage more intimate and meaningful conversation, and I became con-vinced that the best way to nurture great relationships was to provide an element of permanence within proceedings. Sitting around the table rooted people somewhat, but it also gave them a base from which to explore.

After my sighter at The Bleeding Heart, the next dinner I hosted was in the private dining room at Scott's, the venerable fish restaurant in Mayfair. It was very agreeable but a few red flags dissuaded me from returning there. Two missteps by management meant that fresh flowers and bottled water, still and sparkling, were on each table. I did not ask for either but was charged accordingly and it was a valuable lesson to thoroughly check the fine print. Another discouraging factor was the location of the dining room in the basement, since it possessed no natural light. One of the simplest ingredients to create a memorable dinner is windows onto the world; another is the provision of round tables to ensure everyone is in your eyeline.

There are clearly a few practical differences if you are organising a dinner for three hundred rather than thirty. I understand that but I struggle to understand the lack of forethought that compels event planners to place attendees on long pews or behind pillars that both obscure them and limit their visibility. How is that deemed conducive to great conversation? What matters most is that everybody in the room feels a part of the occasion, not just wedged into a corner or trapped at the wrong end of an inanimate and rather tight-lipped table.

I have never encouraged any overt sense of formality at an OFFLINE dinner, as that tends to get in the way of the important stuff. There are no name badges at OFFLINE. I might selectively introduce you to a few people when you arrive or later in the evening, but I am not there to act as a personal chaperone, shepherding your every move. If you happen to forget a name, just ask for a reminder. Nobody will be remotely offended. Should you forget it a second time, ask again and listen carefully. If you need to do so a third time, that particular conversation is probably destined to go no further but one simple trick to keep someone front of mind is to repeat their name back when you are introduced. A bland "Hi" is a world apart from "Hello, Jack," as Jack will far more readily and spontaneously respond when he hears his name. It's a bit like a call to arms.

I have absolutely no desire to ask a calligrapher to painstakingly inscribe a place card for each attendee. That's far too stylised for me. Instead I apply a natural flash of sophistication OFFLINE style by scribbling each name on little blue, yellow or pink Post-it stickers.

There is no rhyme or reason for the colour choice, but the attendees don't know that, and it is always good to keep them guessing! It simply adds another layer of randomness and serendipity.

The invitation to an OFFLINE dinner does not say very much, but that is deliberate. In practice, it starts when everyone shows up and it finishes when they all go home but my greatest priority has always been to create a sense of intrigue and wonder, so I send something along these lines:

> **Please join me and thirty friends and associates at the forthcoming OFFLINE dinner at the Savile Club. It kicks off about 7 p.m. and should be over c. 10/10:30 p.m.—short, sweet and very entertaining.**
>
> **As ever, there will be a suitably eclectic crowd, all ages, all backgrounds, boys and girls. All that matters is that you come with an open mind and a generosity of spirit and, as your host, I shall do the rest. I think you will like it!**
>
> **OFFLINE is designed to encourage fresh ways of looking at the world and the art of sharing. There is neither any agenda nor any outcome, just a bunch of smart, engaging people like yourself who enjoy mixing business with pleasure!**

The Limitations of Conformity

The business dimension at OFFLINE has always been secondary. What really matters is what participants give and share of themselves. The open-mindedness and generosity of spirit that OFFLINE advocates appear to be rare these days. People are often so self-obsessed and wrapped up in their own lives that they make little effort to step out of their comfort zone.

This speaks to a wider problem in society. The desire to conform is very powerful but, all too frequently, people tend to overshoot the runway in the pursuit of validation. The notion of belonging to a group, tribe or value system offers undeniable attractions, but it is the reliance upon it that causes me greatest concern. A silent majority typically surround themselves with those in their peer group who either agree with or endorse their opinion.

The last thing I want to do is host an OFFLINE dinner with thirty people like me because one of me is quite enough! I am drawn to variety and an element of surprise, so I impose no restrictions on the destination of the invitations. It is vitally important too that young and enquiring minds are welcome to challenge the age gap and status quo and, consequently, the ticket price is pitched at a level that addresses the broader market. Occasionally, individuals attended at cost price or in selected cases as my guest if they were truly impecunious, but I felt they would add colour and vibrancy to the evening.

I have a very uncomplicated attitude concerning dress code. Clearly this does require a smattering of common sense, but I leave it up to individuals to apply it as they see fit. The boundaries of appropriateness at OFFLINE are fairly loose, albeit there have been a few startling misjudgements over the years. It's a bit like stepping onto the subway in your underwear. You might pique some interest from your fellow travellers, but nobody will take you very seriously. Women generally do not seek much guidance, but should any men enquire about the dress code, I keep things simple and just tell them that trousers are recommended!

I recall watching a fascinating black and white television clip from *Candid Camera*, probably filmed in the mid-1960s. It featured a fellow awaiting an elevator in an office building somewhere in the US, soberly dressed in business attire, dark suit and tie, white shirt and polished shoes. He is holding his briefcase and hat, and when the elevator arrives, he steps inside and notices three other men there, identically attired except they are all wearing their hats. He can clearly see the fellow alongside him is doing so and, after a few seconds elapse, he arches his back to scratch it. However, he really does so as a means of looking at the man over his left shoulder; he then feigns to pick up a piece of litter to his right and observes that each of them are behatted too. Another ten seconds later, he follows their example and puts his own hat on.

Why is this? Because most people desperately wish to conform and not to draw undue attention to themselves, yet suppressing your individuality is a double-edged sword. Most public behaviour is dictated not by rules but by social convention. There is no government statute I am aware of that unequivocally asserts your mode of dress in a business environment.

A uniform, by definition, removes any individuality and is normally the preserve of large organisations, but it is not always necessary or appropriate. It definitely helps if you are dressed like a fireman when the house is ablaze. It lends a certain authority and suggests that you know what you are doing. However, it matters not that the postman is festooned with Royal Mail regalia when delivering his letters. I am not comforted by the fact he routinely turns up in his regulation outfit. It may help to build a sense of community within the post office, but what do I care? Not a bit. I would be quite relaxed, frankly, if he turned up at my door in flip flops and a Hawaiian T-shirt as long as he delivered my post in a timely way.

As a young man, I worked for a very patrician stockbroking firm and I can remember with great clarity, some forty years later, the incredulity of the partners when one of my colleagues arrived at the office one morning wearing a pair of brown shoes. They could not have been more stunned had they witnessed a lunar eclipse, and their obsession with conformity determined that the miscreant immediately go home and change his footwear. They were governed by a misguided belief that sobriety and convention should be honoured and respected at all costs. I was equally incredulous at their response. His feet would be tucked firmly under his desk. It did not diminish his professionalism. As for those rabble rousers who strayed into striped shirts with white collars and cuffs: Oh, the decadence!

Dress codes in the City took on a different twist with the introduction of dress-down Fridays. This proved an almost insurmountable obstacle for those bankers who had never been confronted by the challenge of dressing as an individual. Some spectacular fashion disasters emerged as, regrettably, creative minds in Latin American debt or asset allocation models were not expressed via their wardrobe. Uniform is more acceptable when a personality is wrapped around it or it merely represents a layer of blandness that reinforces the worst of corporatism. You already know which team you are on so, unless you are playing football, you do not need to wear matching outfits.

Rules of (Dis)engagement

The real revelation for me was that individuals were happy to pay for the privilege of conjoining with similarly bright and diverse characters, whatever their stripe. I was equally blessed by the discovery that my club was the perfect venue to host OFFLINE. The Savile Club was founded in 1868 with a membership originally leaning towards the arts and letters but today encompassing, inter alia, technology, business, journalism, film and music. Additionally, the annual fees are more competitive than the grander gentlemen's clubs, so it appeals to most strata of society, which aligns rather neatly with the approach I adopted at the OFFLINE dinner.

The club is located in a superb townhouse, acquired from the aristocratic Harcourt family in the 1890s by Walter Burns, one of the principals in the JP Morgan banking dynasty, and modified in French eighteenth century style. The building was constructed in the seventeenth century and retains many exceptional architectural features, so there is much to tempt the eye. It has been utilised for product launches, modelling assignments and especially film shoots, as it is one of only twenty private residences in London that still retains its ballroom. Indeed, a recital scene from the award-winning *Downton Abbey* television series was portrayed there. The understated entrance to the club belies a deceptively spacious and lovely setting, which is enhanced by fine food and wine.

There are virtually no ground rules at an OFFLINE dinner, but I do insist at the outset that all mobile devices must be turned off or at least placed in silent mode. After all, I did not send an invitation to your phone to join us! This request is normally met by a sudden flurry of activity, particularly by ladies who struggle to find it deep in the bowels of their handbags. The only other thing I mention is that the room is chock full of talented people, and they should freely explore it and one another.

Should someone pop out to make a call, smoke a cigarette or use the cloakroom, it is a green light to assume that chair should you so wish. The returnee will be obliged to sit at your table so interaction can revolve as much as conversation, but I dislike the policy of forcibly moving people before each course; this should be a natural and organic process. It is most unwelcome while engaged in an absorbing conversation with your table to suddenly undertake a game of musical chairs. The procedure rather more resembles a 1,500-metre race where everybody stays in lane for the first lap and then converges for the following two. The only difference is that at OFFLINE, there are no winners or losers, merely participants.

And what did I talk about? I have long retained a fount of stories in my head based on my personal experiences and observations, whether strangers I encountered, mishaps that befell me or various tales of derring-do, some of which I have recounted in this book. Typically, they pivoted around people, since the human factor was always uppermost in my mind, and the stories frequently revolved around the way we interacted, cultural taboos, conduct, behaviour, manners, kindness and the boundaries of acceptability. But the distribution of articles was an occasional treat rather than a regular feature. I often mixed up the format and, defiantly flying the analogue flag, I also started introducing a quiz into the mix.

A quiz may seem a rather prosaic experience in the eyes of many, but at OFFLINE, it had an effervescent effect. It is vital to devise a quiz that is sufficiently inclusive so that everybody can participate. I was never going to pose a bunch of questions concerning classical civilisation or political speeches or more arcane subjects, as, quite frankly, most of the attendees would zone out. But the first quiz precipitated such an entertaining response from the assembled that I repeated it at the very next dinner to equal effect. It was entitled "The Cultural Life of Cities," and it touched upon places and activities with which they would all be broadly familiar. Yet this quiz and others I created also provided a fascinating insight into what people thought they knew and what they really knew!

Although numerous attendees returned to the OFFLINE dinner over the years, I was continually obliged to harvest new prospects. Where did the guests come from? How did I find them? Which data management programme was I utilising? What lists was I mining? How did I know so many people? I was frequently peppered with such questions, but the truth is that I would speculate to accumulate and did not need to be personally introduced or have known you professionally to start chatting. I was prepared to take a chance, not stand on ceremony, and my instincts were rewarded more often than not.

I had few qualms about levering OFFLINE into a discussion if I sensed an opportunity. For example, if people were a bit obtuse or difficult in a meeting, I might casually mention how much they might learn from attendance at an OFFLINE dinner! I would also conversationally accost others in a queue, in a café, at the football, in passing, wherever, but another weapon in my armoury was that very twentieth-century tactic of using my phone to actually make a phone call. Never underestimate the impact of the personal touch.

In practice, I would initially email an invitation to about 150 people on the basis that perhaps one in five would accept, but I extended it to others in their orbit. Aside from attendees bringing colleagues, associates or significant others in their lives, it often embraced friends of friends and the children of friends. There is no age bar at OFFLINE in either direction. Indeed, last year one friend mentioned he was bringing a companion, and when I casually asked about her name and background, he advised it would in fact be his father! At eighty-six, he was certainly the oldest attendee at OFFLINE but among the most interesting too. After winning a silver medal for swimming at the 1958 Commonwealth Games, he had reinvented himself as an operatic tenor before forging a storied career as an agent in the worlds of music and sport. I am quick to say yes and reluctant to say no and that approach has always underpinned the OFFLINE ethos of displaying an open mind and a generosity of spirit.

At some OFFLINE dinners I would observe certain participants, a little afraid of themselves and their surroundings, tiptoeing around the edge of the proverbial swimming pool. Accidentally on purpose, I might give them a nudge, and they would fall in, but it mattered little whether you entered in the deep end or the shallow nor whether your costume was green or red. The only unifying factor was that you were wet. Nobody in the pool says, "I am more wet than you." You are all wet! Wherever possible, seek out points of convergence, not divergence; there is far more that connects rather than separates us.

The Joy of Randomness

Fishing with a Net

Many individuals go to great lengths to cultivate particular relationships. There is nothing intrinsically wrong with that approach, but I liken it to fishing with a line rather than a net. Sitting on the ideal spot on the riverbank, wearing the right kit, affixing the best bait, checking the weather forecast, the direction of the wind, hoping for a big catch, anglers may get lucky, but they will get unlucky far more frequently. By contrast, I go fishing with a net. I throw the net into the river, haul it in, and see what varieties of fish I have caught. There may be a few fish that are familiar or perhaps of a different colour than usual or that I have not seen for some time. Equally, there may be others that I might not like the look of, and I toss them back in the water! The law of averages tells me that my net will almost always contain a few surprises on the upside and demonstrate the joy of randomness.

And the Schnitzel Came Too

One of the most distinctive pleasures of OFFLINE has been the manner in which entirely disparate connections assumed renewed life after the event. So it proved with Robbie, Chris and Charles. I knew Robbie very well, Chris not very well and Charles not at all. In fact, Charles showed up quite unexpectedly at an OFFLINE dinner with a mutual friend, who was investing in his data company and had brought him directly from a meeting together. I have absolutely no recollection as to how Chris arrived at OFFLINE originally, but he is a shrewd, thoughtful and very likeable Canadian venture capitalist focused on tech prospects in Eastern Europe.

By contrast, Robbie and I went way back, as we had in fact attended the same school as near contemporaries. He is only a year or two older than me, but the usual teenage hierarchies precluded any direct contact, so we only met properly a couple of decades later. After graduating from Cambridge, he immersed himself in the television and film world, notably producing the 2004 movie *The Hitchhiker's Guide to the Galaxy* in collaboration with his close confidant, Douglas Adams. Yet his curiosity and breadth had steered him subsequently towards media finance and management consulting, and I came to greatly respect his intellect, insight and unstinting support for the OFFLINE concept.

All three of them were fascinated by innovation, the benefits and limitations of technology, AI, neuroscience and the rest. They had no prior connection, but I sensed that they all spoke a common language and suggested that the four of us meet for supper at Fischer's, an atmospheric Viennese brasserie and a regular haunt of mine, to see what might emerge. I was not disappointed, as the three of them instantly gelled, and the conversation swayed back and forth. I was largely a spectator, which suited me fine. I just sat back and enjoyed the show, accompanied by my usual order of Wiener Schnitzel Holstein, fat chips and a pickled cucumber salad.

The overall experience was so enjoyable that we agreed to repeat it. Roughly every six months or so, we would gather at Fischer's, where I reacquainted myself with the above combo plus Robbie, Charles and Chris too! At some of our dinners, the world of technology did not appear on the menu at all, but our exchanges were always fun and invigorating, regardless of the subject matter.

Father and Daughter

The impromptu appearance of Charles at OFFLINE was by no means an isolated case. Peter also showed up out of the blue with Bernard, another mutual friend and a savvy antiquarian book dealer, and returned on a number of occasions. Peter is a one-man self-publicity machine, as befits the world's greatest life insurance salesman (or so he tells me!). Immensely personable, he is not a shy and retiring man and cut his business teeth founding the iconic Comedy Store in London.

However, his periodically manic exterior hides a thoughtful and generous interior, best exemplified by his instrumental role in the remembrance in the UK of the 9/11 terrorist outrage by arranging for four tonnes of crushed and distorted girders from the World Trade Center to be relocated to London. They were fashioned into a fitting memorial by the erection of a sculpture now on public display, a vivid reminder that sixty-seven British citizens also lost their lives through this despicable act.

Peter loves to talk, so it is no surprise that he is a regular contributor to the Speakers for Schools programme. He will lend his expertise to anyone who cares to listen, although I believe he has managed to restrain himself thus far from selling any insurance policies to students! But he is always passionate about young people, so it was no surprise either when he brought his daughter Lily, who then worked for an NGO, to an OFFLINE dinner with him. The apple evidently did not fall far from the tree, as she was charming and clever like her father, albeit much better looking!

Peter has an insatiable appetite for conversation, which he has adroitly combined by taking a permanent breakfast table at Claridge's whenever he is in London. Three slots are set aside for his guests at seven, nine and eleven o'clock, and I have always enjoyed his repartee while remaining unscathed from his attempts to sell me life insurance too. Indeed, the only time I have rendered him lost for words is through my routine failure to order the house special of bacon and eggs, as does every other guest, by plumping for peanut butter on toast in a suitably OFFLINE kind of way.

From Derby to Glasgow . . .

Jenny had approached me after reading a profile about me in a newspaper, and she became another devotee of the OFFLINE dinner whenever it coincided with one of her trips to London. She was normally based in Alfreton, a small town in Derbyshire, where she was head of external affairs for Slimming World. Seated to her left at one of the dinners was Stewart, an old associate of mine in the insurance sector, who was shortly retiring to live in a small village in that part of the world, a mere twenty miles away. As he had barely an ounce of fat, he was never going to join the local slimming class, but how strange that they were to become so closely linked geographically.

The interaction between Scott and Sandy might best be described as a fleeting meeting. Scott is an American banker married to Clare, another friend of mine and possessor of the most delightfully mellifluous

Glaswegian accent. As Sandy was bidding me farewell at the end of a dinner, Scott overheard his wonderful Scottish burr and enquired of its roots. It presaged a fascinating conversation on dialects, which was only curtailed by Sandy dashing off to catch his train. This might have seemed unfortunate at the time, but I just viewed it as the prelude to a much more relaxed and diverting conversation, so I invited them to join me for a spot of lunch. One loose connection often imperceptibly leads to others and so it proved again!

. . . to Ethiopia

I am a big fan of Africa. I have barely scratched its surface, but my experiences in both North and South have always been enriching. I have not yet explored East or West, but I kept communing with people in London from that part of the world too and, consequently, I connected Kiki and Baraka. Kiki's bloodlines extended from Kenya in the east to Togo and Senegal in the west, but she had spent much of her adulthood in the US and the UK. In that bubbling cauldron of possibilities called the world at large, she always seeks to build bridges. Although she is involved in fintech, she paints her life across a broad canvas, and I felt she would find many points of convergence with Baraka, a dapper and energetic entrepreneur from Kinshasa who, aside from his property interests, is engaged with the burgeoning Congolese art scene. Unlike Kiki, Baraka had never attended an OFFLINE dinner, although in fairness, Kinshasa to London is a very long way to travel to break bread!

I would occasionally meet Baraka in London, but his trips never seemed to coincide with an OFFLINE dinner, and the three of us never managed to coordinate our diaries for a coffee either, so I simply emailed them both, explained the background and why, as two bright young members of the African diaspora, I believed they would share similar sensibilities. They each acknowledged my note and I thought no more of it. Picture my astonishment some months later when I received a message via WhatsApp early one morning from them. It was a pleasure to see their beaming smiles in the photo but an even greater pleasure to learn that they had literally bumped into one another waiting to board a flight from Addis Ababa at one o'clock in the morning! As one does. When I reflect on defining moments that capture the essence of OFFLINE, this wildly improbable yet serendipitous meeting surely warrants a place at the top table.

The Business of Networking

Let Us Skip the Cake and Come to the Icing

Milling around might have some virtues when networking, but I find standing in the same place is far more effective as the event comes to you; the entrance is particularly fertile ground, as everybody tends to go in and out via the same door! However, the best place to linger is in close proximity to the food.

I rarely arrive at a conference at the appointed hour unless there is a specific reason. Very occasionally, the keynote address might draw me in ahead of schedule or a friend is speaking or, indeed, I am speaking! Ordinarily, however, I aim to pootle in just as the first major session is ending.

As the audience spills out, gasping for air, refreshment, sustenance or whatever, I am there to greet them and introduce myself, fortified by my earlier encounter with the pastry stand. I am frequently asked what I am there for, a particular speaker or theme perhaps, or what I have enjoyed most so far.

I have always believed it is very important to be straightforward in business. So I tell them the truth. I am only here for the food! Some people look askance as if they have misheard me, while others start laughing, often with a mouthful of food, which certainly breaks down a few barriers.

The reality is that very little inside the auditorium is so enthralling that I feel obliged to sit through seven hours of presentations, whatever the setting. Give me a transcript of the salient points of the day and I can read them in the bath this evening instead. I am far too busy weighing up the charms of the brioches.

In my experience, the most interesting conversations are conducted in the corridors, in the gents or over lunch. That is when participants typically drop their guard and their veneer of profession-alism. And that modest voyage of discovery, of course, is so much more revealing!

The Chocolate Challenge

I have learned that there is one surefire way to build rapport when wandering around a trade fair, art fair or similar. My secret weapon has always been to apply the chocolate challenge. Take a big bag of Maltesers and offer them to individuals. Almost everybody likes choc-olate, and that sense of surprise and the unexpected is an energiser. See how those who dismissively brushed past you before suddenly want to be your friend. Who takes one only or delves into the bag to grab a handful. Indeed, who signals to a colleague perhaps to share some too? People reveal their personalities in myriad ways.

Networking is just a fancy word for talking to people. You do it all the time anyway, whether chatting in the queue at the bus stop or waiting at the school gate to collect your kids. Yet a strange mystique has developed around it, as if it is an activity confined to a select few who alone possess the wit, the fluency, the untrammelled confidence to engage and share. There is a perception that networking requires some special qualification or gift to carry it off effectively, but every-body reading this book is an expert at it already. You started as a baby, gurgling in your cot to your parents or siblings. Of course, most of it was complete gibberish, but you generally made a bit more sense by the time you graduated to the playground!

I frequently use the London Underground and notice the dif-fidence and lack of eye contact of those around me, especially on crowded carriages. There is a sense they are softly embarrassed by the awkwardness of being pressed together at such close quarters. But this is where opportunity presents itself. Any exchange with fellow travellers will be transient by nature, unless, perchance, you are both traversing the line from end to end. Should I hear an unfamiliar language in the carriage, I frequently enquire about it. People often have pride in their native tongue and are quite flattered to be asked what it is, as it reaffirms their sense of identity. And even if I have not visited their country, I might be aware of an author or delicacy or landmark from there.

I may sometimes receive a cold shoulder or blank stare but that is no reason not to ask at all. Life is a risk! It reminds me of a conversation after the first coronavirus outbreak with a fellow running trade shows who was justifiably mulling over entry requirements and the need for social distancing. He was concerned about the nature of any physical contact, but I was more concerned that he did not lose his sense of proportion. I did not deny his reservations were valid, but I said that you can insist attendees don masks and gloves and refrain from kissing or shaking hands, but, equally, they can go to the cloakroom, fall down the stairs and break their ankle!

We live in a world where we seek to cover every eventuality but that is not always feasible. You can only take reasonable precautions. There is an overriding belief today that any problem can be swiftly resolved, including a global pandemic, if enough money, technology, resources, time and brainpower are committed. But sometimes there are no solutions or merely bad solutions. The unscripted nature of the chocolate challenge meant I covered no eventualities at all, but it certainly kept me on my toes. If someone brushed me off, I simply moved on to the next, but, as at the OFFLINE dinner, it was all about the interplay of random individuals in unfamiliar territory.

I planned to take that sense of community one stage further by bringing a box of chocolates with me on the tube and offering them to those in each carriage who were displaying OFFLINE tendencies. This clearly ruled out anyone talking on their mobile, scrolling through messages and listening to music or podcasts. However, my plan was literally derailed by the realisation that, if my encounters were to be filmed for wider consumption, I would need to pay a fee to London Underground for the privilege, so I decided to take the chocolate challenge onto the streets of London.

Baker Street, Marylebone High Street and Pall Mall were each busy thoroughfares and offered plenty of scope to tempt any passersby, who were unencumbered by a device of some description, to take a chocolate from the box. It was a little reward for those embracing an OFFLINE life and inevitably drew me into conversation with a wide cast of characters. However, one of the most eye-opening aspects of this exercise was the suspicion from a few people that I had an ulterior motive for doing so. Why did they feel there might be some sinister intent on my part? What did that say about the way of the world today? But there was no catch and their attitude sharply contrasted with the majority I approached who were delighted to burrow inside the box. There were numerous surprises on the upside.

Whenever I offered them to toddlers, there did appear to be a run on the orange creams and praline crunch, but I was all too often distracted by their chatter, and, of course, little hands do burrow particularly deep!

Taking a Chance

About ten years ago, Amit, a US based associate in the aviation business, emailed me to say he was in London and would be pleased to meet for a drink. He asked if he might bring a colleague who was staying at the Stafford Hotel in St James's, a favoured haunt of Americans in London. Yes, I said, whyever not? Who knows where the conversation may take us?! I had no preconceived ideas, but, sitting in the garden at the Stafford, within all of two minutes, it was clear Johnathan and I had a great rapport. Amit was there and not there, slightly on the periphery. The connection Johnathan and I developed was so instinctive and compelling that Amit inadvertently became marginalised by his own introduction.

Johnathan is a lawyer who was appointed head of the Peace Corps in Botswana and retained a tremendous affinity for the country. Always very politically engaged, he became senior director of the National Security Council, organising diplomatic missions for President Reagan, notably his first meeting with Mikhail Gorbachev in Geneva. Indeed, James Baker, foreign secretary in the above administration, was an early backer of a project Johnathan initiated in Botswana. At 225,000 square miles, the country is the size of France, with very modest medical facilities in the bush, so Johnathan pressed sufficient flesh to extract favours and financing to create the equivalent of the Australian flying doctor service there.

Twice a week, doctors were dispatched to regional clinics to assess, inoculate, operate and otherwise, and the service was extended to Zambia and Malawi. It was a tremendous success, all the more so as he actually lives on a farm in Virginia, where he breeds racehorses with his wife. Typically, he used London as an entrepôt to shuttle between Washington and Johannesburg, and he would ping me a text at 8 a.m. to say he had arrived at Heathrow, his connection was leaving at 5 p.m. and was I free for lunch? Often I had an existing arrangement, but I just brought him with! Very few lunch meetings are so personal that another guest is an intrusion, and Johnathan is a smart, understated guy who always adds something to the mix. He certainly leads an OFFLINE life!

Sometimes, if he squeezed in an appointment with a client, he just joined my companion and me for drinks or a quick bite. On other occasions, he kicked back for a while, but either way, I knew he would contribute in a positive and engaging fashion. That sense of randomness can head in all kinds of unexpected directions. Far too often people seek to prequalify attendees at a gathering, as if a failure to do so may result in ghastly consequences. I know your mother told you not to talk to strangers, but now that you are an adult I think you might just be ready to let go of her hand. I took a chance when I originally encouraged Amit to bring Johnathan to the Stafford, and I take a chance whenever I invite him to lunch. It may go no further, or conversely, it may just run and run. Bear in mind that most people are kindly disposed to surprises. Just make them good ones! Everybody has a story in them, which sometimes may be more intriguing than your own, so do not forget to listen well, as a curious and open mind will always introduce new vistas.

Taking Another Chance!

Over a decade ago, I received an email from a close friend of mine in New York City asking for a favour. The daughter of friends in Los Angeles had just graduated from Princeton and taken a role in a sustainable development fund in London. She did not know many people there, and he wondered if I might take her under my wing until she found her feet in the city. But of course. Over the next two or three years, we stayed in touch as she developed her career, but contact grew more infrequent thereafter and largely fizzled out. Evidently, her new boyfriend was far better company than me and quite right too!

Shortly before my departure to a conference in Santa Clara, I was absentmindedly flicking through my LinkedIn account when her profile emerged, stating she was now a business development associate at the Milken Institute in Los Angeles, a nonpartisan think tank that particularly supported initiatives in education and medicine. I pinged her a message and was delighted to learn that she would be free to meet while I was there. She joined me for breakfast at my hotel and disclosed that she was now responsible for organising events and extending the Milken outreach activities. The next Milken London gathering was approaching. Would I like to participate?

London had hitherto been run as a satellite of the Milken operation in Los Angeles, but the organisation had recently appointed a dedicated managing director for Europe. They sought to enhance the core programme with a family office module that included a panel discussion on art. They had already assembled a distinguished roster but they were one short. Apparently, I knew a bit about art. Would I be prepared to join? Whyever not?! Meantime, I was shortly hosting another OFFLINE dinner in London, so I suggested that one of the new Milken team there might wish to attend to broaden their network.

One member of the new team—the managing director himself—did indeed attend. I had never communicated with him before he walked through the door, but I placed him at a table of very diverse characters. His companion to his immediate left never made it, as she was unavoidably detained by a meeting in Geneva and missed her flight, but next along was one of London's top restauranteurs. The two of them really hit it off, forming a close friendship that underpinned collaboration, sponsorship and cross fertilisation between their organisations to mutual benefit.

This specific connection emanated from my desire to assist a young girl slightly out of her comfort zone. She very generously represented me to the Milken Institute as a friend and mentor. I thought I was just an occasional lunch companion, but evidently it had a much deeper impact than I realised. She reciprocated in bundles my initial warmth and interest in her previously. As a past attendee of OFFLINE herself, she reflected its virtues of unconditional giving and sharing to her colleagues.

The tale of Milken and the restauranteur demonstrates that, if you display an open mind and a generosity of spirit, your journey may take you in unexpectedly positive directions. It also reinforces the egalitarian nature of OFFLINE. The most interesting people in life are the most interested and OFFLINE draws together those who have a boundless curiosity in both the world around them and those who inhabit it.

Three for Tea

Good business is all about good relationships and consistently reinforces the power of giving without expectation. The concept of "give
and take" is outmoded. By contrast, if you give and then give again,
the world will open its arms to you, as you will exude trust and confidence, each an essential ingredient to business success.

I arranged an afternoon tea between Basil, Aradhana and Emre,
all friends of mine and past attendees at OFFLINE on separate
occasions. They operated in quite complementary areas, and I had
a hunch they would get along very well. So it proved. OFFLINE
is partly a celebration of the randomness of life as that, assuredly, is
where the juice lies.

The three of them are each engaged in real estate in one form
or another. Basil runs a major property fund sourcing opportunities
on behalf of a group of wealthy families in the US and beyond. He
principally invests in the UK and Germany so, should you ever wish
to learn about the relative charms of Düsseldorf or Cologne, Basil is
your man.

Aradhana is a leading authority in the hospitality sector with a
particular emphasis on tourism infrastructure in emerging nations,
such as Congo and Rwanda. She has played a key role in a number
of hotel developments globally and is a special advisor to the World
Tourism Council, among her many talents.

Emre is an architect who founded a specialist company that
focuses on repurposing embassies and government buildings seeking
modification. Diplomatic requirements are a category all on their own.
You won't find your average ambassador or business consul popping
down to the local estate agent. Embassies bring particular demands
and Emre understands this market conspicuously well.

Amidst the very entertaining and stimulating conversation, Basil
mentioned out of nowhere that he had taken his undergraduate
degree in aerospace engineering at Cornell. Quite how he made the
jump from aerospace engineering to real estate was never adequately
explained but it prompted Aradhana to state she had a connection
with Cornell too.

It emerged that Cornell ran a master's programme in hotel management and that she was an alumna from that faculty. It was a
remarkable coincidence that Aradhana and Basil had attended the

same university. I glanced over to Emre. Surely not? "No," he replied. "I went to Cambridge—but I did attend summer school at Cornell!" What were the odds that three friends of mine with disparate but related interests should be so intertwined? Basil is Canadian, Aradhana is Indian, and Emre is Turkish. They all possessed a connection with Cornell, which is based in New York, yet met in London through OFFLINE.

Polite Eavesdropping

I don't agree with all the rules at my club, but there is one unspoken rule that I agree with very much. Polite eavesdropping is encouraged. Why sit in close proximity to others while staring at your shoes? Behavioural trends are often governed by perceived decorum but obsequiously following the rules does nobody any favours.

One fellow who decidedly goes his own way is Grayson Perry, a brilliant polymath who also happens to enjoy cross-dressing. He is a Turner Prize winner, Reith lecturer and author of a provocative but pithy book entitled *The Descent of Man*, which I highly recommend. He is a man unafraid to speak as he finds but it is his powers of observation that are second to none.

If you are a businessman, your antennae should be permanently attuned to opportunity. I find airlines are often rewarding grounds for unexpected conversations, although a recent trip from New York City to London yielded nothing of interest aside from a spectacularly effeminate flight attendant who made Grayson Perry in a smock look positively butch.

I must say that first class is ridiculously overpriced on aeroplanes. Your vanity or corporate budget might encourage you to turn left rather than right when you board for the dubious privilege of a tablecloth or foot massage, secreted away in your pod, but I will let you in on a little secret. You can pay five times the asking price of coach, but you don't leave any earlier and there is no more or less turbulence!

Flights are a bit like pregnancy. You might endure some discomfort but they are finite. You know when they are going to end. I would far rather pay a modest sum in economy to reach my destination and thus have more scope to secure a comfortable apartment when I arrive. The only downside is that your captive audience on the plane might make you yearn for premature release.

However, when you next lie down on your sunbed at the pool or prop up the hotel bar, please remember there is rarely a perfect moment to strike up a conversation. Nobody rings a bell to signify it! We all need to practise our powers of observation, whether we pick up on accents, table manners, reading material or whatever.

Some of my friends and associates travel quite frequently for business. I am rarely interested in the minutiae of their meetings but much more intrigued as to how they spent their time otherwise, if they had a spare hour or two. Who went to the museum or the zoo or who simply sat at a pavement café watching the world go by, absorbed by all its rich flavours?

When I am asked by prospective guests who else is attending an OFFLINE dinner, I sense they will not make the grade. Serendipity should be celebrated, not cast as a long shadow over the certainty of your life. Far too many people, both in the business world and else-where besides, are far too preoccupied that any exchange should be planned and scripted to avoid any sense of surprise. That is no way to behave. Our very creation was an entirely random occurrence, so why live in a state of denial? The combination of unpredictability and curiosity should never be underestimated.

Role Reversal: When Your B-List Becomes Your A-List

One should routinely reassess relationships to determine if they are in decent running order, not dissimilar to giving your car a regular ser-vice. Yet it is amazing how often this simple exercise is ignored in the world of networking. In practice, your combined business and personal connections are split into three distinct categories: warm, lukewarm and cold. Warm relationships generally embrace family, close friends and your inner circle, people who have seen the best and worst of you over the years and love you anyway. They sit in category one. But you are a known quantity to one another and, although they may be responsive and supportive, they rarely provide a surprise package or sense of the unexpected. Category three is similarly pre-dictable, as it will largely represent the plethora of online relation-ships you have developed, most of whom you will never actually meet in person.

It is category two that yields the greatest possibilities. This encom-passes those with whom you initially established a meaningful bond or rapport but where neither party pursued an enduring connection thereafter. It may be your former golfing partner, your sister's ex-boyfriend or the lady you serendipitously sat next to on the train. Perhaps a retiree from your company with whom you always shared a beer and your mutual love of cricket or that talented intern with a great sense of humour who left for pastures new. These are all examples of individuals who added value to your life at a particular moment in time but where distraction, disruption and distance pulled you apart. The raw materials to nourish those relationships are still present, but they won't move on their own. It requires a demonstrable commitment from you to get them back on track but the rewards are often abundant.

As a broad rule of thumb, category one will not exceed 50 people, while category two, rather more populous, may comprise another 250 or so. Category three you can safely ignore for these purposes, as the risk reward ratio is far less favourable. It is the middle ground that will entice you towards the sunlit uplands of relationships that really count. If only 10 per cent of category two respond to your warm embrace, you will have increased your inner circle by 50 per cent and no doubt enhanced its calibre too. There is so much low hanging fruit out there, yet people often walk straight past the orchard with their eyes fixed on some distant horizon. The newspaper articles I used to distribute were often sent to those in my category two and they acted as a slightly indiscreet pass or prompt on my part. Some never responded to my overtures, but plenty more did, and those connections have been cross fertilised to great effect in their turn. In addition, you will find many natural givers among their number, precisely the people whom you should be cultivating anyway.

It's the Culling Season

Once upon a time, life was very straightforward. All your associates, business or personal, were written down in your address book. If it became full, you replaced it, but at least limitations of space ensured a measure of quantitative control. Alas, the profusion of social media platforms encourages the reverse effect today. I have just learned, moreover, that a few people on LinkedIn have reached a ceiling of thirty thousand connections. That is the size of a small town! I have no wish to build a contact base of that scale. Indeed, I am heading in the opposite direction, abetted by happenstance on two separate occasions.

A beautiful thing occurred when my LinkedIn account was hacked. I received a message from the company stating that another email address had been applied to my account and that I should remove it if it was unauthorised. Sadly the message did not disclose how I might accomplish that task, given my own email address had been compromised in the process. Every effort to log in was disabled. My email address was not recognised by LinkedIn. I had no way to contact the company directly, as there was no twenty-four-hour hotline winking at me across its website. There was, no doubt, a method to potentially resolve the issue, if I managed to navigate the labyrinthine help pages, but I had neither the time nor the patience to do so.

Consequently, I signed up as a new member with a completely different email address and password and bumped into myself along the way. There I was, profile intact, photo too, all articles I had written present and correct, except I was now Johnny No Mates. The rogue emailer had stripped every single one of my contacts but, rather like an opportunistic burglar, took everything in immediate view and left the valuable stuff behind. Do you really want all my connections, many of whom are not real connections, not OFFLINE connections? Be my guest. I don't know who most of them are. I estimate perhaps 20 per cent are those with whom I would like to build a substantive long-term relationship. Some I know anyway, OFFLINE style, in the real world. Less is more.

Frequently, random users would ask to connect with me on LinkedIn. If I liked the look of them or they had an interesting story to tell, I would typically accept, regardless of whether I perceived a direct benefit. I ignored the majority, as I tend to apply a rule in which I envisage myself observing people in the foyer of a hotel. Most might just receive my raised eyebrow or tilt of the head as a tacit acknowledgement, but there are always a select few with whom I think I might wish to enjoy a quiet drink at the bar. If the bond is especially strong, I might even, in exceptional cases, invite them to my room but there are plenty more I am delighted to wave off from the foyer on a long road to nowhere in particular! That rather reflected my LinkedIn experience, which is truly a mixed bag.

I had a parallel experience when my old iPad finally expired and went to its eternal rest in mobile heaven. As I had only intermittently backed it up, virtually all content that really mattered was wiped clean. But I discovered that my email accounts were alive and well and my articles were retrievable too. The only thing that was lost without a trace was my address book with some nine hundred contacts. You might think disaster but I spied opportunity. How many of those nine hundred were truly valuable to me? I concluded that roughly one-third represented people I knew and liked, all close friends and associates, a second third those with whom I enjoyed an occasional relationship, while the final group substantially comprised people I either could not remember or never much cared for in the first place!

My email trail acted as an aide-mémoire to those who frequently corresponded or engaged with me. I reasoned that any omissions would find me through other means if they wished to reconnect, but I lost no sleep over it. I just sought to maximise those relationships that were truly reciprocal and meaningful. It largely ran in parallel with my approach to redefining my LinkedIn contact list. Although it has been hijacked of late by a bunch of refugees from Facebook et al., who should really have stayed at home, LinkedIn is unashamedly business orientated and that brings its own drawbacks. In my experience, many financially prosperous people suffer from a syndrome called high extrinsic motivation. They are often emotionally insecure and seek acceptance and validation from the endless trappings of wealth, whereby they are more concerned with the recognition of others than direct benefit to themselves. Conversely, those with high intrinsic motivation are emotionally secure and derive satisfaction primarily from connection and community.

Rebuilding my address book from scratch proved very cathartic. The top hundred were easy to determine, the second hundred slightly less so, the third more problematic. I congratulated myself on my emphasis on quality over quantity, but almost inexorably, my contacts sailed through the five hundred mark and beyond. Whisper it quietly, but it is now around fifteen hundred, and I feel another cull is due, this time by my own hand. One of my cousins revealed a few years ago he had over seven thousand names, many of which were duplicated, so his address book was morbidly obese. I suggested to him that no more than 10 per cent of those names were required to forge healthy business relationships. You would never find a real address book of that magnitude unless it was the size of *War and Peace*.

Managing your contact base online should encourage a certain tact. Nurture relationships with care and handle those that matter with courtesy. This may seem a rather quaint approach to many, but it is of critical importance. I recall my four-year-old son making a beeline for a curly-wurly at the newsagent and, when asked to show the shopkeeper his appreciation, stated, "Thank you, Mr Man," a sentiment I echo by saying, "Thank you, Mr Hacker Man!"

Unless you are fanatically well organised, managing your connections requires discipline and care. Your online persona is an adjunct to your relationships in the real world, not a replacement, so a periodic cull of your address book is a healthy and natural process. Streamlining your affairs brings clarity and focus while allowing you to concentrate on those relationships that really matter, both old and new. If you write down annually on a sheet of paper all those people, in business and beyond, who are important to you, it may surprise you as to whom you remember and, indeed, whom you forget! The wider issue is that hacking is an invisible and corrosive threat, not easily countered, so the very best antidote is to ensure you keep salient information in your head and embrace an OFFLINE life. Your brain is one piece of technology that nobody can take away from you.

Corporate Schmorporate

Shuka, Rattle and Roll

When I first met Pumela, I was wearing a shuka. I had never worn one before, and, moreover, I was wearing it in front of over one hundred people at a dinner, the vast majority of whom I had never seen before in my life. The occasion was a fundraising affair on behalf of a charity, run by my friend Sonal, which aimed to support the education of young girls from the Masai Mara in Kenya. Traditionally, girls did not receive much formal education, as they were frequently betrothed once they reached puberty, and the nomadic lifestyle of Masai herders meant they were never in one place for long.

Sonal is a very smart Indian lady with East African roots. She originally made her mark as a specialist in credit risk before becoming a therapist and displayed other attributes in developing a boarding school almost from scratch on the Mara. Her efforts had yielded assistance from Sir Richard Branson of Virgin and a few other compassionate donors, but the charity Educating The Children suffered from a low profile, so I suggested she create a fundraiser to build greater awareness. I roped in my friend Aradhana, as she was well connected, involved in hospitality and very engaged in female empowerment, and the dinner started to take shape.

As the planning stepped up, a quasi-committee emerged. The subject of dress code started a particularly animated discussion. I was quite happy to attend in a regular business suit, but there was a strong body of opinion that, given the occasion, there should be greater formality. The preponderance of women on the committee encouraged the idea that a couture gown was the only way to go and, if so, men should be decked out in black tie. Unless, of course, they would be attending in national dress.

There were a few African dignitaries coming, and certain tribal chiefs, I was assured, would be so attired. I was rather looking forward to learning their fashion tips, as the Africans have a style all their own. Indeed, I was reminded of the phenomenon of "les sapeurs" in the Congo. This group of men, often of very modest circumstances, celebrate their individuality by dressing as flamboyantly as their budget and imagination would allow. It is showmanship in its purest form.

I had no desire to display my sartorial choices by dressing in a black tie. A business suit was more than adequate, but I was overruled on this point, and one of the assembled, seeking to be helpful in a spectacularly unhelpful way, suggested that if I did not wish to wear black tie to the occasion, I could always come in national dress and complement the African contingent. To my consternation, the entire committee thought this was an exceedingly good idea, but I comforted myself that this would not be a complete disaster if I simply mingled with fellow guests. I would be lost in the crowd. Nobody would notice me.

It then dawned on me that Sonal had asked me to host the proceedings. So it was that everybody noticed me, including Pumela. Aside from my shuka, I was also decked out in an *enkewara*, a huge beaded necklace, and sundry Masai bangles and bracelets. My immediate priority was to ensure my shuka, a sort of wraparound tunic, did not shimmy loose as I greeted guests. I experienced no undue alarms as my shuka held firm during cocktails but, as I stood there addressing attendees before dinner, I let it all hang out. I was surely the first portly, greying, white Masai warrior they had ever witnessed. But I was undeterred, and so were they.

My ensemble was a momentary blur as, once they had adjusted their eyes, they then focused on the message from Sonal and me about the vital work of Educating The Children. We raised over £35,000 through the exceptional generosity of sponsors and guests alike, while my evening was enhanced by the honour of wearing the prettiest frock of the night. And then Pumela approached me to host an OFFLINE dinner on behalf of her organisation, Brand South Africa. Whatever was she thinking?!

The Gift of Mandela

I knew of Pumela previously through David Stoch, a talented pub-
licist whom I had retained for OFFLINE. He told me she was a
very dynamic woman, a real force of nature who had been a protégé
of Nelson Mandela. She was now the UK director of Brand South
Africa, the marketing arm of the South African government, and was
a huge advocate for her country. Pumela was especially keen to share
its story beyond the diaspora, and as I knew a plentiful cross section of people in London, she enquired if I might curate a dinner on
behalf of Brand South Africa.

It all sounded good to me, albeit David did proffer a word of caution on more than one occasion. Pumela, he averred, was a passionate
and charismatic speaker but, once she got into her stride, there would
be no stopping her. She would be unlikely to respect the clock and
confine herself to the allotted period. Would I be able to rein her in?
What a delightful problem!

I suggested to Pumela that I would speak before and during dinner and that she would have the freedom of the room thereafter. She
arrived in a blaze of colour, wearing the resplendent African fabrics
that were such a part of her signature style. We touched briefly on
what she might say but I left it to her judgement. I shared a few stories
over the evening from the OFFLINE playbook and also distributed
envelopes to all attendees as a going-home present. Each envelope
contained articles on aspects of South African life and culture as a
further reminder of the attractions of the country. It just made it a bit
more personal.

I curated six dinners for Brand South Africa and, although Pumela
often varied the content, there was one element that she always featured. On the very first occasion, unbeknown to me, she regaled the
audience with the favourite poem of Nelson Mandela, a source of
great strength to him during his long incarceration. The entire room
was gripped by it as she sashayed around the tables and I insisted she
repeat it at every subsequent dinner I hosted. The power of these words
and the feelings they induced had an electrifying effect.

There was a seriousness to her core message about the prospects
for South Africa, but when she was not enthusing about farming pro-
ductivity or other matters of state, she liked to have fun. I did not
discourage her. Picture thirty-five or forty guests, regardless of age,

status or background, on their feet engaged in a bout of African dancing, pogoing up and down together. Or the time when she displayed her full repertoire of clicking sounds, part of her Xhosa heritage, and invited everyone in the room to follow suit.

Pumela loved the OFFLINE ethos and asked whether she might attend a dinner in a private capacity rather than on behalf of Brand South Africa so she could enjoy the occasion without needing to perform. "Of course," I replied. On the day of the dinner, she called to confirm she was coming, which was great news. She then informed me she was bringing a companion, which was not quite so great, as the dinner was completely sold out, and I had already nailed the table plans. But I liked Pumela and Brand South Africa was an important client so, as a matter of courtesy, I asked her about the background of her companion. She told me Sello was a very good friend, only in London for three days and excellent company. It also transpired he was the CEO of the Nelson Mandela Foundation. "Oh," I said, "I think we might just squeeze him in!" There was always one extra chair available at a dinner in extremis—mine!

The Gift That Kept on Giving

Sello was, indeed, a remarkable fellow. I barely spoke to him at OFFLINE, as there were so many distractions at the dinner itself, so I made a point of meeting him properly the following day over a cup of tea. His upbringing had certainly demonstrated his tenacity, self-belief and humility. It also caused me to ponder over my own circumstances: the comforts of home, the unspoken benefit of white privilege, the ease and convenience of so many things I took for granted. None of these were available to Sello as a child.

Sello told me that he came from a poor family in one of the Johannesburg townships. He never knew his father and out of six siblings, only he and one of his sisters were still alive. He had been raised by his mother, an illiterate domestic worker who had done her best under straitened circumstances, but he unquestionably endured a very challenging start to life. One salvation for Sello was that he was a studious boy who thrived at school. It was his dream to go to university but there was little chance of fulfilling it, as the fees were quite beyond his reach. Although he took part-time jobs to supplement the family income, his savings were too modest. He then discovered upon matriculation that he might qualify for a bursary whereby, if he could raise half the sum required himself, the government would contribute the balance.

This transformed his prospects, but it was still not quite enough. He was explaining his predicament to his mother and wondering how he could make up this shortfall when his blind grandmother, lying upon the stone floor of their shack, snatched him from his moment of despair. Overhearing the conversation, she said that she did not know why he needed the extra money but that she recognised that it was important to him and, consequently, she would give him her monthly pension as his family's contribution to his future.

Sello said that his grandmother had no concept of what a university was or how it might offer him a platform to climb out of poverty. But she knew that it mattered to him and that was enough. I remember thinking to myself that this selfless gesture had unwittingly propelled one of the finest South Africans of his generation into such a critical leadership role. Each time I share this story, I am deeply moved by the actions of his grandmother, who never witnessed the fruits of her investment but assuredly played her part in his ultimate success. Small things can often make a big difference, but their impact is frequently overlooked.

Accidental Networking

I wrote an article on LinkedIn that drew a very warm and appreciative response from Anna. She revealed that she was an artist and had been approached by a radio station in Bristol, where she lived, to talk about her work. Although flattered to receive the invitation, she had never expressed herself through that medium before and was extremely nervous about the show. In the hours preceding the show, seeking some kind of distraction, she randomly alighted upon my article and drew strength from my observation that if you spend your life scared to make a mistake, you mistake your life. The interview proved a great success, so much so that they planned to ask her back on a future occasion. She was thrilled and kindly dropped me a line to thank me for inspiring her to be bold and trust her instincts. I responded that I was pleased I was able to assist her in a modest way and that I would be delighted to meet for a coffee if ever she was in London.

It turned out she was coming there in a mere four days and wondered if I might be free, despite the short notice. "Are you free this Thursday evening, as, by coincidence, I shall be hosting an OFFLINE dinner?" I asked. She happily accepted the invitation, but on the day itself, at about 5 p.m., she called me unexpectedly. I presumed that something had come up and she could not make it. On the contrary, she advised she was very much looking forward to meeting me and everyone else and that she would be there with her husband. At this point, I did not know she was married nor that she had planned to bring Martin with her but, as ever, I improvised the seating arrangements, and they had a fabulous time. Indeed, they so enjoyed it that they returned subsequently and I got to know Martin quite well.

We would occasionally meet for lunch as, although his home was in Bristol, he was based in London for part of the week. He was a senior account executive at Salesforce, a very substantial cloud computing platform for customer relationship management. Given my undisputed status as a Luddite, I really had little clue as to what exactly he was selling but Martin was always good company and also a keen proponent of the OFFLINE philosophy.

Around this time, I was toying with the concept of a corporate version of OFFLINE to help organisations expand their profile and reach. I had created a draft pitch document that outlined the benefits of pursuing such an approach. As I was running late for a lunch appointment with Martin, I thought it would happily occupy him while he was waiting for me. He understood the OFFLINE formula and I thought he would be a sound judge of the efficacy of the idea. Once I arrived and we exchanged the usual gossip and pleasantries, he told me that he liked it very much and asked what I would charge to curate such an event on behalf of Salesforce.

The Value of a Good Lunch

I quickly scanned the proposal and I realised that I had omitted one of the most critical components—the price! This required me to think on my feet. I did not wish to charge too much and scare them off or too little and not be taken seriously. So I plucked a figure out of the air that I instinctively felt would be fair and reasonable. Martin did not flinch or appear unduly concerned and told me that he would speak to his events and marketing team. By the end of that day, he confirmed that they agreed in principle to my proposal and wished to proceed.

Like many technology companies, Salesforce struggled to demonstrate a truly personal touch and wanted to get closer to its clientele without selling them anything. I recommended that they should invite around twenty management, customers and suppliers and I would ask a similar number from the OFFLINE universe. Their invitees included Goldman Sachs, Nielsen Media Research, GVC, the sports betting platform, and a few smaller businesses. I explained that my lot would likely be a motley crew and, moreover, I offered no assurances that any of them would be remotely interested in Salesforce products. But the dinner was not about Salesforce or OFFLINE; it was all about how their people connected with my people and their respective satellites beyond. That was where the value would lie.

Devising table plans is always an entertaining exercise, especially when you don't know half the attendees. I had plenty of fun playing with the permutations, which inevitably carried a speculative element. This can, of course, work to great advantage, and so it proved with Steve. At the time, he was the marketing director of *The Economist* and, as he confessed to me later, he had little idea about OFFLINE except that the magazine had been asked as a guest of Salesforce; he was free that evening and had accepted their invitation.

He explained that he routinely attended many events on behalf of *The Economist*. They were intellectually stimulating and largely populated by the minds that mattered but the programme was always tightly managed. Virtually every gathering was accompanied by biographies of the speakers and a detailed agenda. It was polished and professional but choreographed to within an inch of its life, and there were no surprises. By contrast, OFFLINE appeared to follow no discernible plan. Steve mingled with other attendees over predinner drinks and he was then dispatched to his table, where he discovered the fellow to his left managed a hedge fund while the lady to his right was a piano teacher. As for the chap sitting directly opposite, he ran a dog-walking business! Nobody much cared about Steve's role or status at *The Economist*, but they were far more animated about his life and his passions. Indeed, he found the whole experience so refreshing and liberating that he returned to future dinners independently.

Part Two
Codes of Conduct

The Masters and Misses of Management

I recall reading a newspaper interview with Gerry Robinson while he was CEO at Granada. He was a very shrewd, understated Irish accountant brought into the company to weld its disparate interests together. Inter alia, Granada owned a substantial contract catering business with some twenty-five thousand employees spread over fifteen countries, and his interviewer suggested he must work all hours God sends. "On the contrary," he said, "I work regular hours, as do all our people. Obviously, if we are closing a deal or we must handle a particular problem, our people will stick at it until it is sorted." That is the way it should be, but I am not impressed by people who routinely work sixteen hours per day, as if it represents some kind of badge of honour. And, naturally, if you are routinely working those hours and popping into the office every other weekend, it means you have no sense of balance or proportion to your life. You do not spend enough time with your partner, your children or yourself. It is a rather selfish life. It is a bit different when it is your name over the front door and you are fighting hard to keep your business alive but, if you are in paid employment or engaged in the professional services sector, it suggests you have your priorities all wrong.

Winning Kindly, Losing Graciously

Winning can be measured in various ways. Being first is one way among many, yet people have become conditioned to think that supremacy, physical or otherwise, should be placed on a pedestal, above every other quality. Vulnerability has many charms. By contrast, there is a harshness to "winning." It is sharp and it is finite. It is also adversarial. If I win, you lose. By contrast, "success" tends to suggest a team effort, collegiate and inclusive and emblematic of progress, not conquest. There is no end game. Success is ongoing. Listen to your pronunciation of each word. How does each roll off your tongue? And then spell out each word by hand as if you were sitting opposite someone. *WIN* is angular, full of straight lines. *SUCCESS* is wavy, warm and lush. It is an inviting, luxuriant word. The water is warm and you just want to dive straight in. Winning is like taking a cold shower. It's effective, but I don't want to linger there.

Why are many business leaders so serious or grumpy? Because in their march to the top, they almost always forget to take that one essential travel accoutrement—a cushion! When they are surveying their kingdoms, they are sitting on one of the pointed edges of *WIN*, and it's very uncomfortable up there after a while, especially when no colleagues can easily ascend those long stalks to keep them company. The slopes of *SUCCESS* offer a more gradual incline and allow you to help one another towards the summit. You can even stop by for a coffee and pastry en route and I will happily join you to discover what you have learned along the way. Conversation tends to be an afterthought when climbing that pole. You are so focused on retaining your grip on it that you forget to reach out and engage with those beneath.

Losing is generally disagreeable, but it is rather more palatable if you are at least able to acknowledge the skill and quality of your opponent. Harbouring a grudge or a lingering resentment that you have only been undone by outrageous misfortune or the connivance of others is a childish attitude. Your opponent may be your competitor, but he is not your enemy nor the source of unreasonable hostility nor the target of a blood feud. Yet the ability to concede graciously, whether losing a transaction you thought was in the bag or being beaten in a game your team had dominated, is paradoxically a mark of success. Sometimes one must accept that the fates have conspired against you and the cards of life fell a certain way at a particular moment.

John Wooden, the revered American basketball coach, possessed an acute understanding of what really made people tick. A trophy-laden career encouraged his keen appreciation of the nuances between success and winning. He stated, "Success is like character. Winning is like reputation. Your reputation is what you are perceived to be; your character is who you really are." Despite their outstanding ability, his teams were never concerned with winning alone. There was a way of winning and it was defined as much by the selflessness and camaraderie of the group as by any sporting prowess. They inspired confidence and loyalty in one another. They practised more intently and enjoyed doing so, but above all they were bound by a set of common values. Play fair, play hard, and, indeed, play to win, but never at the cost of your personal conduct. Wooden expected a display of magnanimity and the hand of friendship to always be placed centre stage, whether on the basketball court or off it.

Can Leaders Change Their Management Style?

The challenge for many leaders is that the command-and-control approach of yesteryear must now be delivered with a side serving of empathy and empowerment. Can leaders change? Of course they can. But do they want to? That is another matter altogether. Change of culture, company, expectation or otherwise invites scrutiny of accepted practices on both sides. Leaders, typically, like to be right, so the process of adaptation best suits those who possess sufficient vision and breadth to be inclusive. Occasional hints of vulnerability can be highly attractive, as they are indicative of an authentic personality. Nobody likes a smart-arse who has all the answers, so a dose of humility and weakness from leaders can be very enriching for all concerned. Strength for its own sake has its limitations.

Martin Roth, former director of the Victoria and Albert Museum, arrived from Germany, tripling visitor numbers in the process, but his success reflected three qualities that transcend sector or specialisation: confidence, power and affability. Much depends on the relative robustness of a given company. Roth inherited an organisation that was fundamentally sound but punching below its weight. A forceful, coercive approach was not required. The platform was not burning, but he needed to inject vigour, creativity and self-belief across his team. A combination of Teutonic pragmatism and British cultural programming led to record-breaking exhibitions on themes as varied as David Bowie, Alexander McQueen and the delights of engineering. His exuberant personality and ambassadorial qualities, as well as his ability to adapt to market forces, were the pivot to energise the museum.

Antanas Mockus displayed leadership of a markedly different quality as mayor of Bogotá. Innovations included being filmed in his shower to show the virtues of intelligent water usage and introducing 420 mime artists to minimise traffic misdemeanours, believing that gently ridiculing motorists rather than merely fining them would encourage a change in behaviour. What else might you expect from a mathematician and philosopher?! His counterpart in Medellín, once one of the most dangerous spots on the planet, transformed his city by running cable cars from the favelas directly into the central districts. A change in leadership style was driven by necessity, as the authorities recognised that investing in people and infrastructure in the poorest areas would allow Medellín to gain a collective sense of pride and purpose. Leaders do not require knowledge of all the facts, merely those that enable them to make key decisions.

The Defects of Being Strong

You may not swiftly recall Mark Malloch Brown, but I remember him for two very good reasons. In his capacity as deputy secretary general of the United Nations under Kofi Annan, he openly criticised American foreign policy and incurred the righteous indignation of John Bolton, the American ambassador who seemed to regard any such remarks as a private diplomatic matter and not one to be shared with the unwashed public. Aside from that little tiff, I recall him for his perceptive observation that great leaders also know when to follow and, in so doing, he delivered a telling statement on the ways of the world.

Leadership and its acolytes seem to be everywhere these days. I read so much about strength of character, strength of conviction and strength of purpose, but for many people, their strength is their weakness. There is an apparent inability to recognise that strength for its own sake is not necessarily an asset. I happen to believe, by contrast, that weakness, applied in the right circumstances, has huge value. When people demonstrate weakness, they in turn demonstrate humility, and when people demonstrate humility, they learn to listen. Too many are too quick to offer an opinion and do not spend enough time listening, reflecting and considering.

Of course, one can go too far in both directions. Excessive weakness can induce passivity and a tendency simply to roll over or fall into line. Should you be obliged to egregiously display your loyalty to a person or cause you dislike, take comfort from the old Ethiopian proverb that declares that when the great lord passes before him, the wise peasant bows deeply and farts silently. I feel those who have a need to reinforce their strength also reveal their insecurities either by dominating others or through a refusal to accept they may be wrong. Additionally, there is an inclination to think that experience always knows best, but experience per se is often overrated. It is only truly valuable when it is cumulative. If someone tells you they have twenty years' experience, you need to determine if that is one year's experience twenty times over or perhaps four years' experience five times over. One year of experience repeated twenty times is not recommended. It is rare indeed to find leaders who are able to share the fruits of their wisdom based on twenty years of mixed experiences, lessons learned, forgotten or remembered.

Think Differently

A little subversiveness or radical thinking in the corporate environment can be very beneficial. I attended an investment conference in Paris a few years ago, and, although I have a hazy memory of its actual content, I do remember my sense of deflation when I registered my arrival and was handed an iPad. What purpose did it serve? I was in the room. I was alive. I was awake! Yet that was not quite enough. Apparently, the provision of an iPad would enable participants both to minutely follow proceedings on stage and to pose questions to the panel, should they deign to accept them. This was a prime example of Death by PowerPoint.

As a bare minimum, I expected to see an open forum whereby attendees could at least stick their arms up to challenge a point of view during these sessions, but not through this bloodless, sanitised experience. Even more lively and entertaining would have been the provision of an empty chair on stage to invite individual delegates to randomly join in aspects of the conversation with the experts. Instead, we witnessed a formulaic approach that showcased an event bereft of any spontaneity. Not a good look and definitely not OFFLINE.

Another example of slightly stunted corporate thinking came from a prominent law firm in London. One of the partners was a fan of the OFFLINE concept, and she wondered if I might curate an event on their behalf. We had some interesting conversations about the path they wished to follow but one particularly struck me. They arranged an annual garden party to draw together clients during which perhaps three partners from different areas of the practice would speak about the activities of the firm. I felt this was a missed opportunity.

These partners were a known quantity to most clients, and the occasion should have acted primarily as a platform for some of the rising stars, those maybe a notch or two below partnership level, to share their insights and personality with the guests. It would raise their profile and confidence in a very public manner while simultaneously emboldening the belief of the clientele that the future of the firm was in excellent hands. That would be a truly progressive move, but the safety-first option seems to be the prevailing mentality when hosting events. In other words, ignore any innovative thinking and avoid cock-ups. The law firm seemed to like my idea very much, but not quite enough, as, regrettably, they chose to pursue other options!

Both organisations are highly regarded by their peers and possess a justifiable reputation for the quality of their advice. Yet they also symbolise the inertia and fear of so many protagonists in the professional world. They all need to inject a little devilry into their wider interactions, and an essential piece in their armoury should be a bench in their foyer designed by Droog, the famous Dutch design collective. Their playful creations will club any sense of self-importance out of the ballpark, and the bench, brilliant in its simplicity and effect, exemplifies this. It is an unremarkable metal structure with an indentation on its surface just deep enough to contain a variety of marbles. On top of the marbles are placed a series of dinner plates that, whenever the sitter adjusts position, sway across the surface! You thought you were being directly addressed by the CEO until his plate skittered across the marbles a couple of feet to your left. Just the thing to keep him on his game and inject a little levity and humanity into proceedings. Visual gags can be very powerful. I toyed with the idea of introducing wigs, red noses and Groucho glasses for attendees to wear at an OFFLINE dinner. You might look at that executive a bit differently if he is seated opposite you in an Afro or with a drooping moustache!

What Football Management Teaches Us about Life

It is questionable whether outstanding football managers have the credentials to run major operating businesses too. Of the most recent crop, Arsene Wenger and Sir Alex Ferguson, erstwhile leaders at Arsenal and Manchester United, respectively, were supremely versed in man management and the consistent ability to reimagine and integrate new teams over a prolonged period. Wenger was an economics graduate who became a pioneering coach in France and latterly Japan, an urbane but slightly obsessive man who implemented his vision for Arsenal with a forensic attention to detail. Equally, Sir Richard Greenbury, former CEO of Marks & Spencer and an ardent Manchester United fan who subsequently joined its board, stated that Ferguson would be extremely well equipped to run a corporation if he had the right support act behind him.

Among other things, Wenger presided over a revolutionary approach towards diet, stretching and training techniques in English football with due single-mindedness and proceeded to create teams of uncommon poise and power. Yet his professorial and avuncular air belied a fiercely competitive spirit that he shared with Ferguson, who gave a hint of his own leadership qualities when he was elected a shop steward at nineteen in the tough Govan shipyards in Glasgow. Each man displayed a patriarchal tenderness towards his flock, although both, especially Ferguson, were capable of splenetic rage and ruthlessness towards the incompetent or insubordinate. But they also knew how to build dynamic, free-flowing teams and weld the component parts to best effect.

Unlike Wenger and Ferguson, who were players of middling talent, Brian Clough was a gifted centre forward, recently capped by England, whose trajectory was pointing firmly north when he suffered a devastating knee injury. Modern medicine would have rebuilt his knee, but in 1962 it beckoned the end of his career. In his late twenties, with few savings to fall back on and a young family to feed, he took on a lowly managerial role and climbed from there to the very pinnacle of his profession. Clough was an opinionated and outspoken man with a firm view about the style of the teams he coached and, moreover, the way his players conducted themselves. He famously sent one player home ahead of a flight to a major European fixture for not being clean shaven and another who failed to bring his club tie. Needless to say, both rushed back in time to catch the plane, but it was a lesson from Clough in maintaining standards and personal values!

After defying all expectations and leading unfancied Derby County to the title for the first time in its history, he took up the reins at the similarly underperforming Nottingham Forest, a division below, and repeated the trick. Clough possessed an almost unshakable conviction in his judgement and was not averse to haranguing club directors, fellow managers and the press if it suited his purpose. Yet his viperish tongue and beady-eyed control ensured his teams were very sporting and had few disciplinary problems; he inspired fealty and fear in equal measure.

One of the most memorable instances of Clough in action was illuminated when he was doorstopped at the training ground by an enterprising reporter from one of the Nottingham newspapers. The young man tentatively approached him. Apparently, Clough had a reputation for being autocratic and simply riding roughshod over the opinion of others. Was this true? Clough bridled at the suggestion and stated that his door was always open to players, directors or staff. If they had any points of issue, they were invited into his office to express their opinion, whereupon Clough would express his opinion and then they would both agree that he had been right all along! He did so with a smile but with just a hint of menace, inferring that anyone who dared to cross him would be unlikely to do so again.

His managerial record speaks for itself, but his attitude and demeanour are sadly replicated in business and public life today. All successful men (and indeed women!) come with their own complexities, but some disguise them more subtly than others. Wenger and Ferguson brought a joie de vivre to the game, whereas Clough, frequently hectoring against authority, railed against it. There was always an edge, perhaps a lingering resentment his career had been snuffed out while he was in his prime. Yet he was an articulate man, often witty and perceptive, who was twice approached to stand as an MP by the Labour Party and twice declined the opportunity. His brash and forthright manner did not diminish his genius as a manager, but his abrasiveness, especially during his slow descent into alcoholism, would probably have rendered him incapable of passing any corporate governance test!

The Quality of the Experience

Apple and Aga are two retailers who get it right. Why? Because they have focused on the quality of the experience rather than the purely transactional element of selling. The best retailers of the future will not utilise much physical space to sell anything but create an environment where customers wish to linger. What parallels exist with museums where a fair proportion of visitors spend time in the café or bookshop rather than stepping inside the resident collection? How can they feed off each other? What lessons might high street stores learn from that?

An apple was green and red and round when I was growing up. I don't recall ever consuming a square apple, and yet I have written this book on one. The square version has become ubiquitous today, but twenty years ago, it was just another vaguely technology-related brand. But that all changed for me one blisteringly hot afternoon in Pasadena, home of two of the finest art institutions in California, namely, the Huntington Collection and Norton Simon Museum. I had visited the former in the morning with my friend Mike and, after a highly agreeable lunch, we planned to check out the latter too. We crossed the road so we could walk in the shade but took a most unexpected detour en route. Most stores on Colorado Boulevard displayed fairly conventional facades, so when we alighted upon a conspicuously bright and glass-fronted establishment, I felt strangely compelled to peer inside.

The first thing that caught my attention was that the staff were each dressed top to toe in white, all tanned and impossibly good looking. This was not the only surprise. There were a cluster of desks equipped with minicomputers, iPods and the like that actively encouraged browsing. The staff were suitably upbeat in a Californian kind of way: they were helpful to a fault and invited people to wander at leisure, ask questions, perhaps watch an online seminar about the product range. It transpired that I was standing in one of the very earliest Apple concept stores, a space imaginatively designed to be welcoming and inclusive, but the most startling aspect of all was that there was no obvious means to buy anything!

No doubt if you absolutely insisted on a purchase there and then, they would place an order to the warehouse in Nebraska or wherever, but there was no overt emphasis on selling. It was all about nourishing the quality of the experience and, aside from the excellence of their present array of technological baubles, they maintain a similar standard today. The brand awareness of Apple now inhabits an altogether different plane, but my diversion in Pasadena was a valuable insight into the triggers that bring people together.

Aga is another innovative company that has placed an accent on the quality of the experience. In some of its larger showrooms, there is a fully fitted kitchen at the back with a separate entrance that contains a variety of stoves for customers to try for themselves. The kitchen is equipped with all the usual accoutrements plus a long refectory table upon which a basket is placed. And inside that basket you will find an envelope with $200 cash and a note from the company inviting you to go shopping for dinner at their expense and not to forget to pick up a couple bottles of wine en route. Once you return, you can experiment on the different stoves as you prepare dinner for the eight guests who will be joining you around the table. Given a stove can retail for $10,000, this $200 outlay is a clever and seductive method by which Aga can build goodwill and, of course, gain access to other possible purchasers sitting around the table and participating in the experience.

Many years ago, I met a senior executive from Christie's auction house for breakfast at their very grand premises. Aside from the usual cares of business, I was especially interested in the development of its profile in the world beyond. So I asked him to envisage what a Christie's megastore might look like, a place of business where there was no business. Where would it be located? What packaging would be created around the concept? How would the narrative share the story and draw in those ingénues who would never ordinarily dream of setting foot inside a saleroom?

Why do you not find a hip, fashionable restaurant on the ground floor of a major bank or law firm? It is such an obvious place to generate business in both directions and becomes a destination point in its own right for the company. Inevitably, the working environment will be reconfigured in the postlockdown era, so offices will need to be reimagined to ensure the quality of the experience encompasses rather more than mere technological finery and a smart address.

The Charms of Imperfection

Walk the Line

One theme deeply embedded within the OFFLINE philosophy is the charms of imperfection, which might reasonably be described as a celebration of being a bit crap. And let's face it, we are all crap in our own sweet way! However, as Mark Twain, the American humourist and writer, teasingly remarked, success has a thousand fathers, yet failure is an orphan. People are often exceedingly quick to claim credit for their positive contributions, however modest, yet strangely reluctant to acknowledge their weaknesses.

Nowhere was this more glaringly displayed to me than a few years ago when I attended a conference in Santa Clara, California. Although the conference focused on marketing and communication, I learned plenty else besides. The first thing that became abundantly clear, if ever there was much doubt, is that America is one of the world capitals of shouting, although the Germans, Israelis and Italians would surely give them a run for their money. Americans seldom convey themselves in a regular voice; instead, they boom and they project. Indeed, I had to remind one fellow that I was standing in front of him and not on the other side of the mountain!

The conference provided affirmation too that Americans suffer from a very severe dose of hyperbole whereby almost everything is exaggerated to frankly ridiculous proportions. Words like *stunning*, *amazing*, *incredible* and *awesome* routinely littered the conversation. Even more evident was the abiding interest among delegates in the concept of business mastery, the pursuit of excellence at all costs, always striving to the nth degree towards a slightly unattainable goal. But what is wrong with being very good, or quite good or just better than last year? Why is it that unless you punch out the lights and reach for the stars, you have sold out, you are not serious, not a professional? Really? Nobody told me!

The most interesting speaker at the conference was a fellow named Roger Love. His name meant nothing to me, which proved something of an oversight on my part; as it transpired, he is arguably the finest singing coach in America. He has worked with a plethora of leading performers, including Madonna, Michael Jackson, Earth, Wind & Fire, and, most recently, Eminem. I was tempted to ask whether peanut or plain, but somehow the words got stuck in my throat.

Meantime, Love had extended his repertoire into the world of public speaking and never had breathing technique been quite so fascinating to me. Apparently, we all express ourselves through our head voice or our chest voice (though I did wonder whether he had deliberately omitted our posterior voice, which often speaks more vigorously than either!). Yet the most revealing aspect to me was a story he related that demonstrated how perfection and imperfection can quite happily coexist without us being any the wiser as to which is which.

He was sitting in his studio one evening at his home in Los Angeles when he received an urgent call. The man at the other end was very agitated and declared that he had a major problem. He was producing a film called *Walk the Line*, a biopic based on the life of country singer and songwriter Johnny Cash. The team had just cast Joaquin Phoenix as Johnny Cash and Reese Witherspoon as his wife, June Carter Cash, and belatedly discovered that Joaquin Phoenix was tone deaf and unable to sing a note! Reese Witherspoon was also tone deaf and had not sung since she was fourteen in the school choir. The producer stated that Love had come highly recommended, and he enquired about his availability. Filming was due to begin in a month. When could he start? They would pay whatever it took to retain his services. And so a few days later, once his fee had been wired to his account, he was whisked by private plane to meet the crew and actors on location.

Roger Love explained that he was unsure quite what to expect. How bad could they be? These were professional actors, after all. Surely they could adapt and improvise, as required? The answer quickly became clear. Very bad indeed! Reese Witherspoon was not an immediate problem, as she was a reasonable singer and had a lesser part. Joaquin Phoenix, by contrast, required Love's complete focus, so he started by emphasising the five key components of voice—pitch, pace, tone, volume and melody. Once Phoenix understood these principles, Love set to work, solidly, intensively for that month. Each time he coaxed a perfect tune out of Phoenix, it was stored digitally. He spliced the component parts from each track on his computer thereafter so that they effectively appeared as one long string. Utterly seamless.

And I thought to myself, wow, how extraordinary to see the lengths people will go to attain perfection. How good does it have to be? Should Joaquin Phoenix miss a bar or three because he was playing with his quiff, would anybody actually notice? Or feel that the film was undermined as a consequence? Surely not.

Perfectionists are competitive with themselves before anything else. There is a competitive gene within all of us fighting for attention. For some people it lies largely dormant, while for others, it can be tremulously active, but there is a tendency either way to overlook those aspects of our personality that may appear a little unsavoury or blemish a superficially perfect record. Yet we should recognise and celebrate our deficiencies and weaknesses, as they are not an indelible stain on our character, merely a reminder that we lead an authentic life. If you bring together the world's fastest athlete, most beautiful woman and finest intellect, you will find that, regardless of their outstanding individual attributes, their lemon soufflé always collapses at the vital moment. Keep it real. Here are five more examples of imperfection in action:

You earned $47 trillion last year but still can't tie up your shoelaces. Very well done!

You just broke the land speed record but always snort when you laugh. Masterful!

You speak nine languages but always forget faces. I bow at your feet!

You are stoic in adversity. And then you have a little cry. Let me kiss your hand!

You are a bloody marvel. Except when you drop the ball. Another special gift!

Cross the Line

There is arguably no finer example of the charms of imperfection than the marathon runner who kept coming in last. Each year, *The Sunday Times* produces a compendium called the "Rich List," detailing the presumed wealth of the great and the good and the not so good. In one edition, the "Rich List" incorporated a feature, sponsored by Škoda, on citizens globally who led rich lives, whether contributing to their own community or wider society. Amidst a number of remarkable and inspiring individuals, one particularly caught my eye, a woman in America who professed herself to be an avid marathon runner. She declared she had competed in over one hundred races and on precisely twenty-six occasions, she had finished last!

Why was that? Because she valued her social capital most of all. She was never going to win the race; she was not interested in beating her personal best and you certainly wouldn't find her pounding the pavement at 5 a.m. in preparation for the big day. Instead, she would hang with the back markers, those perhaps participating in the marathon with a disability or recovering from an operation or running in a silly penguin costume to raise money for charity—all stragglers in the race, perhaps, but gold medallists in life. They shared the experience, conversed while jogging, engaged with the crowd, gloried in the freedom from expectation and built a mini mutual appreciation society along the way. If they chose to sit down after fourteen miles to share an orange juice, they would do so. If any race observers were agitated by this apparent deviation from procedure, they revealed a great deal about their own insecurities. What particularly drew me towards this woman? She was obviously warm and compassionate but, even more importantly, she was a giver.

I was frequently asked what kind of people attended OFFLINE. What criteria did I apply? And most alarmingly, did I do any vetting? The reality is that I did not much care where people came from—their occupation, age, ethnicity, sexuality, income or religious disposition, for example—but I cared very much that they were givers, open and curious, interested in fresh ideas or perspectives and, most of all, interested in the lives of others.

Far too many people grapple with the burden of expectation that ensures they are presented in the best possible light. But why sweat the small stuff? How dull to be obsessed with winning and the adoration of your peers. It is our shortcomings that best define our individuality, and we should celebrate them accordingly. Our weaknesses and inconsistencies should be considered an accompaniment, not an impediment, to leading an OFFLINE life. Mark Twain would surely approve!

Beyond the Line

Sporting glory has never paid me the compliment of a personal visit, so I have enjoyed it vicariously through the achievements of others. I have happily flirted with mediocrity, as any whiff of competence has been fatally undermined by my twin lack of talent and application. Unless you play a sport professionally, I think it should always be fun but I am not saddled by an overtly competitive streak in that regard.

I sometimes spot people running in the park or the street. Are they late for an appointment? They have barely got dressed! Do they give me a wave and smile? Am I tempted to join them? Not at all. Almost invariably they display furrowed brows, puffing, grimacing or incessantly checking their stopwatch to measure their steps and time. Where is the pleasure in that? Is it not enough just to be outside, breathing in fresh air with nature all around?

I knew a business associate many years ago who was an excellent golfer. He played off a handicap of four, which placed him in the upper echelons of the amateur game. I casually asked him about it one day, and he told me he was no longer playing. Had he suffered a bad injury? Had he been expelled from his club for some indiscretion? Was he unable to afford the green fees? On the contrary, the reason he had stopped was because he was not getting any better, and if he was not continuing to improve, he no longer wished to take part. But what about your playing partners, the banter, the scenery? I told him that not all his faculties were in decline. He could still remember his scores, see the flag and walk around the course! But he was adamant that he would pick up his clubs no more and that was that. What a sad conclusion to his sporting life.

I have never had to contend with the prospect of sporting decline. As with most aspects of life, it is important to manage your expectations. I always hoped to ameliorate my performance on the tennis court but never at the expense of my enjoyment. I used to strut my stuff with a coach every Sunday and we became quite friendly. Heath was a very accomplished player who had won many tournaments as a junior and represented his county but, on his own admission, was just a notch or two below the level required to make a good living on the professional circuit. By my lowly standards, he was a veritable genius on the court and it was always a personal triumph when I managed to win a point through my own efforts rather than a mishit or occasional double fault on his part.

Heath told me that he coached a few Australians and South Africans and that they were ultracompetitive. When he entered the court, they were already undergoing their stretching routine and sundry preparations. And they took themselves terribly seriously. They would knock up beforehand with such a relentless focus and intensity that by the time they started the match itself, they would run out of steam, and he would easily pick them off. But I presented him with a different kind of challenge.

I certainly did not cut much of a dash on the court, despite the presence of my Green Flash plimsolls, so far out of fashion they had come back in again. As Heath gathered the balls, there were no admiring glances, no heads were turned, there was no hush of anticipation, although that was partly because I had not arrived yet. I generally turned up a few minutes late, and, after taking the acclaim from precisely nobody, we began our prematch ritual of discussing the football results and interesting films that had just been released. The warm-up never made much discernible difference to me, as my eye was never truly in, so we quickly got down to business.

We had some excellent rallies, best perfected by me when the ball was in close proximity and landed with a comforting plop near my feet, and I did strike a few winners over the years that astonished me, let alone Heath. But these were fleeting moments, a cresting wave in my sea of sporting mediocrity. After an agreeably loose-limbed half hour, during which Heath had noticeably broken neither sweat nor stride, I suggested we pop over the road for a coffee and sticky bun to dissect the bones of my performance. There actually wasn't much to dissect, as my performance was reliably inept, but the bun certainly slipped down a treat. How can one possibly deny the charms of imperfection?!

However, as my exploits in the field may be justifiably viewed as inertia personified, I always greet tales of extraordinary sporting endurance with a mixture of awe and wonder. The awe is simple enough, but the wonder is how bonkers some people are. There are myriad cases of individuals fulfilling long-held ambitions by testing their physical limits, and Maud Fontenoy demonstrated this point in spades. As a slight, slender woman of twenty-seven, she sought to show that size and strength alone mean little without mental toughness and resourcefulness. Her achievement? Rowing seven thousand kilometres across the Pacific Ocean on her own in seventy-three days while variously contending with a broken seawater filtration system and diving into shark-infested waters to fix her boat. Spending the first fifteen years of her life at sea was certainly a handy start but, nonetheless, it's a pretty staggering feat. As for my feet, you can rest assured they remain rooted to the spot.

Nuneaton Borough—Pride of the Midlands!

The late Pope John Paul II opined that football is the most important unimportant thing in the world, the kind of penetrating insight that surely propelled him to the top job at the Vatican. I have been privileged to attend many wonderful matches at the highest level, often flecked with both finesse and sweet brilliance, but I have derived much pleasure too from watching the journeymen of the game, who often play for the sheer love of it. They will rarely achieve the status of the top professionals but, nevertheless, they display a passion and commitment to the cause that is mirrored by their supporters.

Wherever you watch a match, you can be reasonably assured that, measure for measure, the travelling supporters will be the noisiest and most fervent bunch in the stadium. Yet it is one thing to crisscross the land following a relatively successful club but quite another to do so for an outfit in the lower reaches of the game. But I have witnessed teams of lesser ability over the years, notably during a weekend visit to Lancashire for a charity dinner at the behest of my friend Catherine. Before I arrived, I asked if she could procure a couple of tickets for a local game. However, no professional club within a twenty-mile radius had a home fixture for one reason or another, so our options were confined to non league matches. Thus my partner Frederique and I were instead entertained by the contest between Chorley and Nuneaton Borough in the National League North, six rungs below the Premiership.

And what a thrilling and uplifting affair it proved both on and off the pitch! The game finished 2–2, albeit I only managed to see the first goal, scored in the opening minutes by the visitors and on a wrenchingly bitter day the clubhouse offered warmth and sanctuary at halftime. Somehow word got out that we lived three hundred miles away and were attending this low-key match, despite having no affiliation with either club. The Chorley archivist felt compelled to share its history via the photographs on the wall and when I expressed more than a passing interest, he sought out his scrapbook to show me his cuttings too. As he did so, I saw the bar gradually thinning out as spectators were returning for the second half. While he swooned over the past exploits of the club, I started politely to edge my way towards the door, and, as I did so, I heard a throaty roar of approval from the crowd. Chorley had already equalised! I missed the third goal too, as my view was sadly obscured by the stanchion, and the fourth at the very end when we were leaving the ground. Our host, a friend of Catherine's, had an appointment immediately after the game, so I was denied the injury time drama too.

The reverse experience occurred a few years earlier when I attended a game between Hampton & Richmond Borough and Maidstone United and only witnessed the last goal. My son Rube played for Hampton juniors from the age of five or six, and although he subsequently moved to other teams, we both retained an affection for the club and decided we must one day see the senior team in action. When that day finally arrived, Hampton were punching slightly above their weight, as they had only recently been promoted, and Maidstone were the league leaders, so there was much to look forward to. Alas, we left home a bit late and then became snarled in a terrible traffic jam near Kingston Bridge, so by the time we finally walked through the turnstiles, half an hour had elapsed, Maidstone were three up and the game was effectively over.

But the game itself was just one piece of the pie. One of the joys of non league football is that you can wander around unrestricted. Segregation of supporters is a bit meaningless at this level, since there are so few of them in the first place, but Maidstone brought a tidy contingent, some fifty strong, all bedecked in the yellow club colours and in fine voice. Half time was an opportunity to fraternise with the locals and I lingered rather longer than I should probably admit in the caravan in the car park that doubled as the club shop but, inexplicably, Rube was rather more preoccupied with the aroma of barbecued sausages on the griddle wafting in our direction. I protested that this was no time to be snacking as he led me empty handed to the queue. But it was not a moment to quibble, as the overall experience was the epitome of the grassroots movement that brings communities together. Hampton pulled a goal back in the second half to reduce the arrears and, although it did not change the outcome, the joy that greeted it was music to my ears.

Amidst the endless quest for excellence and self-improvement, we often lose sight of what is most important. Sadly, progress is not always progressive and there is a virtue in the simplicity of life. You do not always need to attend a West End theatre to enjoy fine acting or a Michelin-starred restaurant for great cuisine or, indeed, a heavyweight clash to experience exciting football. The Hampton players may have been performing on the fringes of the professional game, but they could certainly run faster than me, head the ball in the right direction, trap and pass it with one peg and often two while showing some real flashes of quality, all of which I much appreciated when I was not absorbed by the programme notes, so respect where it is due.

But I convey my greatest respect for an undeniably OFFLINE moment at Chorley where I saw two opposing supporters in glorious isolation holding up a massive banner for the duration of a freezing first half emblazoned with the battle cry "Nuneaton Borough—Pride of the Midlands!" This had not been acquired from the online shop but painstakingly, if inexpertly, created at home over many hours and no doubt schlepped to every away game over the season to a set of footballing backwaters. The standard on the pitch or in the clubhouse might leave something to be desired for those fixated by the superficial glamour of the top clubs, but the welcome and sense of kinship at this level would always be warm and genuine, a feeling to be loved and nurtured.

Spreading the Word: Lessons from the Demise of Robert Mugabe

Social occasions bring many unexpected challenges. Can I eat the canapés without spilling them down my shirt again? Who is this person in front of me with a strange name? And why is nobody dazzled by my fetching trouser suit? I pressed it myself! They may be further complicated in a business environment where you might have to contend with divisive or dictatorial colleagues. Will she ever shut up? Why on earth do we need to be there each time at eight on the dot? Why was I only on the provisional list? When will this ever end?

And when hosting events, how long should you talk to keep the audience engaged? How sensitive are you to your audience? When hosting OFFLINE, I speak over the course of the evening, but more than once, I have not bothered with the last leg as people were having such a good time. Who am I to interfere with their fun? After all, I am the least important person in the room. Every host should remember that, but Robert Mugabe clearly had a terrible memory. Like Donald Trump, he forgot the simple truth that he was in power to represent all interests, not merely his own.

How sensitive was Mugabe to the expectations of his people? Ruling by fear is no way to run any organisation, as you simply advertise your weakness. What matters is how you treat the lowest common denominator, not the highest. Mugabe surrounded himself with sycophants who agreed with him at every opportunity out of a misguided sense of loyalty. Did he spread goodwill and any concern for the man on the street? Only accidentally or for the cameras. His high opinion of himself was shared only by a few outside his inner circle.

The charms of imperfection enable you to demonstrate a more rounded personality. When you do not hide your weakness, you display humility, and when you display humility, you learn to listen. We were given two ears and one mouth for a reason and they should be used in due proportion! Moreover, acknowledging your weaknesses invites others to show complementary strengths, unless you suffer from a severe dose of paranoia and consider the state to be your personal fiefdom. Recognising the qualities of your opponents, even if you disagree with or dislike them personally, is the mark of a leader. Rapport and empathy play their part, yet Mugabe dismissed them out of hand.

Mugabe turned Zimbabwe from the breadbasket of Africa to the basket case of Africa through breathtaking economic incompetence. Other African potentates have sat in the hot seat with grim records for even longer, such as Biya in Cameroon and Obiang in Equatorial Guinea, but they did not squander the resources and infrastructure that Mugabe inherited in Zimbabwe. He never offered anything other than a cursory acknowledgement of an alternative view. Those who disagreed were eliminated from the equation. He failed to listen and, consequently, lost all trust.

By contrast, Nelson Mandela showed the virtues of giving without expectation. He led by example and, despite his years of incarceration, demonstrated his respect for difference. He was by no means perfect, but his demeanour, consideration and sense of fairness always prevailed. When you give and then give again, you magnetically draw people towards you as they want to share your goodwill. Mandela was also a fine communicator, whereas Mugabe was merely in love with the sound of his own voice. Indeed, he was so arrogant that, even as a nonagenarian, he did not think to groom his successor.

He ignored a few other basic business principles too. It can be unwise to marry your secretary; one might kindly describe Mrs M as a gold digger or unkindly as something unprintable. Mugabe completely lost his grip on reality once she entered the picture.

Additionally, you should constantly keep your ear cocked to the voices of your people, as your audience is everything, and remember that even a broken clock tells the correct time twice a day. Evidently, Mugabe should also have attended an OFFLINE dinner to see where he was going wrong! A blind focus on the pursuit of perfection at all costs is a foolish endeavour. You will never achieve it and just think of the agonies along the way when it always slips just out of reach. In a personal context, I am a firm believer in the 80/20 rule, which states that if 80 per cent of your life is sufficiently good, you learn to accept the 20 per cent that is not. When the numbers appear in inverse proportion, you know it is time for a change.

The Courtesies of Life

It's Just a Feeling

When you reflect upon defining moments in television, the screening of the 1969 US Senate Subcommittee on Communications might not instantly spring to mind. Yet it contained a brief presentation so powerful and so persuasive that it changed the face of educational programming for children forever. It was delivered by an extraordinary man named Fred Rogers, who dedicated his entire career to nurturing communication skills among young children. He principally addressed his remarks to Democrat senator John Pastore, chairman of the committee, and it was quite a sight to see this brusque, hardnosed operator melt as he listened to the smooth and measured exposition of an expert at the very top of his game.

Rogers had been invited to make his case as part of a pitch by PBS to obtain greater federal funding to support its initiatives. At that time, programming for children was dominated by action rather than thought. There were numerous examples of showdowns at the saloon, madcap horse rides, men in capes and questionable headgear, fighting, explosions and conquests—plenty of doing but not much thinking and even less feeling.

As a boy, Rogers struggled with loneliness and an inability to express his emotions freely for fear of causing offence or behaving inappropriately. His personal experiences encouraged his belief that all children should be reminded that they are special in their own way, that they have their own voice and that they are appreciated just the way they are. This philosophy was ultimately crystallised by the creation of a television series, never since replicated, entitled *Mister Rogers'*

Neighborhood. It was a platform that advocated openness and warmth, but it was never patronising.

Rogers was on the level with all the youngsters watching and explained in simple terms the value of thoughts or feelings. His fundamental decency was perhaps best illustrated in the clip where he talked on set to a young boy named Jeffrey Erlanger, who was a quadriplegic. Rogers asked him about the electric wheelchair he used, but he did so both sympathetically and directly, and watching the smile on the face of this very bright and brave child was a moment to treasure. It was no surprise to learn that they remained in touch over the next twenty-five years.

I imagine that Rogers would have rubbed along very happily with Dale Carnegie, author of that seminal book *How to Win Friends and Influence People*, who was driven by similar principles. Rogers may have stepped onto a rudimentary set, but his language and delivery were of the most sophisticated kind, a masterclass in simplicity. Trust and confidence are among the key building blocks of life and Rogers implicitly understood the way they should be conveyed to his youthful audience.

In a wise and perceptive interview with the journalist Charlie Rose, he described himself as an emotional archaeologist. He meant that he was gently probing those hidden recesses tucked away in the psyche of the child. Rogers believed that fear or anger or misunderstanding should not be ignored or suppressed and he provided an outlet for his young viewers. He was a man with an innate goodness about him, which he transmitted on screen. In every episode of its thirty-three-year run, he greeted his viewers with a warm smile and proceeded to change his jacket and shoes while facing the camera. This ritual was both constant and reassuring and it was always accompanied by a little ditty in which he invited each child to become his friend and neighbour.

Another classic in this genre that emerged contemporaneously was *Sesame Street*, which was hippy, zippy and slightly frenetic, awash with colour and movement, and the two programmes resembled siblings who, despite possessing the same DNA, looked and sounded utterly unalike. Abetted by the puppet wizardry of Jim Henson, creator of the Muppets, *Sesame Street* was as focused on doing and thinking as feeling. By contrast, there is almost a contemplative air about Rogers, who, whether stroking week-old chicks or feeding his fish tank or amiably chatting to other members of the cast, invited his viewers into a personal conversation.

He was especially concerned with exploring affective behaviour around themes such as emotions, relationships and ethics. What does divorce mean? Why did the Space Shuttle *Challenger* explode? Why must I get a flu jab from the doctor? Big and scary things need explanation. Children are too smart to be routinely shielded by half-truths and shoddy language. Not knowing or understanding allows fear to fester and this fear can lead to hatred and bigotry. Their intuition is often quite pronounced and should not be ignored. Reaching out to them in an accessible way, he gave them permission to share their vulnerability. I do the same thing whenever I host an OFFLINE dinner.

In his testimony before John Pastore, Rogers stated, "We deal with such things as the inner drama of childhood. We don't have to bop somebody over the head to make drama on the screen. We deal with such things as getting a haircut or the feelings about brothers and sisters and the kind of anger that arises in simple family situations. . . . I feel that if we in public television can only make it clear that feelings are mentionable and manageable, we will have done a great service for mental health."

Rogers possessed a homespun, whimsical air and could easily have stepped straight out of a Norman Rockwell canvas. Indeed, he became such an American icon that one of his knitted cardigans, a permanent fixture in each episode, is now on display at the Smithsonian Institution in Washington, DC. But there was also a steeliness about him, deftly camouflaged by his soothing and thoughtful tone. He was appalled by the bombardment on television of animated violence, pie throwing or mindless activities largely devised to obtain laughs at the expense of others.

Despite its slightly knockabout style, there was also a serious underlying message to *Sesame Street*. It was exported across the globe through a slick marketing machine and concomitant licensing deals, which have contributed to its longevity, but this was an approach Rogers eschewed. In fact, he balked at any overtly commercial activities that might deflect from his modus operandi. One director commented that if you took all the elements that make good television and do the exact opposite, you would have *Mister Rogers' Neighborhood*! But he was an outlier then and he would be an outlier today, as the appetite for incident and sensation has not abated. Who or where is the twenty-first-century heir to Fred Rogers? Over the hills and far, far away.

It is no surprise that Carnegie's most successful title has remained such an essential text because the lessons he shared within have a timeless and universal quality. Like Rogers, he understood that the key to building great relationships is making people feel good about themselves. Confidence and self-esteem are delicate flowers that can wither or bloom to remarkable effect. Acting with civility and kindness is the springboard with which to develop meaningful long-term connections in all walks of life. These are also lessons I have sought to apply to the OFFLINE concept.

Despite their superficially staid exterior and demeanour, each man displayed a slightly subversive streak. Carnegie placed a strong emphasis upon the social skills to build confidence with peers, especially in a business context, but he also devoted a section in *How to Win Friends and Influence People* to seven rules to create a happier home life. Most of the usual suspects are represented, such as not criticising your partner, being attentive and appreciative, but an unusual addition was his recommendation to read a good book on the sexual side of marriage. This advice was certainly a departure from business primers in 1936, when it was first published, and Rogers complemented this forward thinking in his own particular fashion.

One integral member of his cast was a young Black actor named François Clemmons. Racial segregation sadly still remained prevalent at this time in America, so Rogers subtly pricked societal prejudices by inviting Clemmons to share his foot bath to cool down on a hot day. It was a lesson to his young viewers that we are all the same, just a bit different, and it was a lesson to himself to practise what he preached. Before he started his career in television, he had qualified as an ordained minister, so his sense of faith and family conflicted with the realisation that Clemmons was gay. Yet he acknowledged that Clemmons added his own qualities and that he was as special in his own way as any of the individual kids enjoying the programme. This blend of emotional intelligence and pragmatism in thought and deed marked Rogers as a man of acute sensitivity, and it also explains why his relationship with Clemmons endured long after the latter left the show.

Authenticity is a rather hackneyed term these days, but Carnegie and Rogers both demonstrated it splendidly. Carnegie described himself as "a simple country boy" from Missouri, but his self-deprecating manner masked a fine mind and a genuine desire to help people communicate better. He made his name initially as a lecturer in public speaking, but his homilies on life rather resembled those of a psychologist. Carnegie declared that "any fool can criticise, condemn and complain, but it takes character and self-control to be understanding and forgiving," and those words resonate even more strongly today. If you find room in your heart to acknowledge the strength of difference, your life will be immeasurably improved. Seeking a means to diminish or pillory others to gain advantage merely advertises your own weakness and self-interest.

Rogers considered that one of the most important parts of any book was the white spaces between the paragraphs, as they enabled the reader to think, although this rather metronomic approach to life is at odds with personal entertainment offerings today that continue to prioritise sensation over silence. We inhabit such a noisy world that a conversation of pauses is an alien concept to some. Yet Rogers and Carnegie displayed an uncommon nexus of networking and mindfulness, and despite their methodologies and language appearing a little dated today, they contain many pearls of wisdom within. Like a couple of magnificent perennials, they have stood the test of time. They flower across every season, and OFFLINE pollinates their seeds in its own distinctive way, scattering them to the far winds.

110 Rules of Civility

As a fourteen-year-old boy, George Washington transcribed *110 Rules of Civility and Decent Behaviour in Company and Conversation*, a set of maxims based on the writings of French Jesuits in 1595, entitled *Bienseance de la Conversation entre les Hommes*. Given the tender years of Master Washington, I think we can make allowance for his variable spelling and the use of capitals and reflect upon the fact that these lessons are as relevant now as they were then. Here are a few examples:

25. Superfluous Complements and all Affectation of Ceremonie are to be avoided, yet where due they are not to be Neglected.

56. Associate yourself with Men of good Quality if you Esteem your own Reputation; for 'tis better to be alone than in bad company.

70. Reprehend not the imperfections of others for that belongs to Parents, Masters and Superiours.

90. Being set at meat Scratch not neither Spit Cough or blow your Nose except there's a Necessity for it. [It seems the vegetarians got off lightly there!]

100. Cleanse not your teeth with the Table Cloth Napkin Fork or Knife but if Others do it let it be done wt a Pick Tooth.

109. Let your Recreations be Manfull not Sinfull.

110. Labour to keep alive in your Breast that Little Spark of Ce(les)tial fire Called Conscience.

The Jesuits were great believers in the idea of *cura personalis*, which broadly translates as the care of the individual, a view that sits comfortably alongside the precepts of Fred Rogers. Those Jesuits certainly got around. Another youthful adherent of their teaching and a contemporary of Washington was Toussaint Louverture, the famous Haitian slave who rose to free five hundred thousand men and women from bondage in Hispaniola through his wit, acumen and leadership skills, frequently accompanied by a splash of his voodoo heritage. It was the Jesuit leader Ignatius Loyola who coined the epithet "Give me a child at seven, and I shall give you the man," and I believe that civics is a subject that should feature on every school curriculum. It has too often been dismissed as an indulgence that does not render any useful qualification in the thicket of examinations and grades that are conventionally applied to define a successful life.

I have a friend in the US who, every year, sends all her associates, both young and old, a copy of the powerful and deeply affecting "Letter from Birmingham Jail," composed by Martin Luther King Jr. after his arrest in 1963. He very eloquently shared the struggle for acceptance and equality in the Black community, but his words today transcend any racial bias and address the fundamental desire for civil discourse across almost all strata of society. As a descendant of slaves himself, he was cut from a similar cloth to Toussaint Louverture and was quick to remind his audience that civility was not about manners per se but respect for difference.

I Disagree, but You Are Arguing!

There is a major gulf between a disagreement and an argument. You and I may disagree on many things. You may recommend a brand that I think is overpriced or overrated, while I may think my football team is superior to your own, but these are merely differences of opinion. It does help if your counterpart can put you down in suitably classy fashion, as did my friend Michel to me. We were having a vigorous and somewhat heated debate on a matter of a footballing kind whereupon he turned to me and bluntly stated, "Howard, I think you are talking bollocks but at least it is quality bollocks!"

However, an argument is an escalation of a disagreement whereby people take a very entrenched position to justify their choices and struggle to find a way to back down graciously if they are challenged. One does not need to apply excessive decorum to make a point, but one should allow the co-conductors of the conversation to express their voice without being drowned out by background noise. People often display an impatience to reinforce their stance and shout down the opposition, so their invective becomes harsher, snarkier and more intemperate. There is a primordial instinct to get in first and stay in first as if any delay places you at an instant disadvantage. The American author and academic Jonathan Rauch shared a wry but keen observation about his own father, who was historically prone to sudden and irrational bursts of anger. His father became far calmer and at ease when, as Rauch put it, "he stopped having five-dollar reactions to five-cent provocations."

This kind of overreaction is a misstep that is all too often repeated. Concentrating upon and listening to your counterpart is vital to any constructive dialogue. By definition, a dialogue is a conversation between two people as opposed to a monologue where you are talking to yourself. If you are unable to listen and bide your time, you do both parties a disservice. The Dalai Lama expressed this view very cogently when he remarked, "Many people think that patience is a sign of weakness. I think this is a mistake. It is anger that is a sign of weakness, whereas patience is a sign of strength."

Table Talk

About twenty-five years ago, I was chairman of a company undergoing rapid expansion and I was invited to offer a second opinion on prospects for senior management roles. They were all professionally capable, but I was far more interested in their personal rather than technical attributes. However, conducting an interview in the board-room brings its own limitations. There is a kind of protocol and order of play in such conventional surroundings and I wanted to take them out of their comfort zone.

Consequently, I would ask selected individuals to join me at a restaurant near my office for a spot of lunch. It was a good restaurant, although it was often busy and no booking was permitted, so you might be obliged to share a table. I was far less preoccupied with their track record or the composition of their CV but wanted to learn what made them tick. There were two questions I always posed: What are you bad at, and what are you reading?

Some seemed genuinely appalled at the idea they could be bad at anything, which instantly set alarm bells ringing, as did those keen to impress upon me the range of their business reading. This was under-whelming news for me, as I was much more attracted by those who stretched themselves in unfamiliar areas. I recollect one fellow who told me that he just did not have time to read, given the demands of his clutch of small children, but every night, he would religiously do the *Financial Times* crossword in the relative sanctuary of his bath. This was a very respectable answer that demonstrated that he was prepared to stretch his mind in unfamiliar territory and was also scrupulously clean!

Once we sat down, who said please and thank you to the waitress and, moreover, looked her in the eye while addressing her? Who had dirty fingernails or a stain on their shirt? Who asked their neighbour alongside to kindly pass the salt rather than lunge across the table for it? There was nothing definitive about any of my observations, but they all gave me an insight into the character of the individual. My lunch guests often demonstrated their talents in unexpected ways. Indeed, I remember one fellow whose sonorous voice carried him beyond the hubbub of the restaurant and I thought he would certainly capture the attention of others. However, he did not capture my attention elsewhere, and our conversation went no further.

It is very enlightening when you take people out of their comfort zone. Some may freeze, while others may rise to the occasion. Who is adaptable or curious, and who responds favourably to uncertainty? Of course, my own judgement might be a little awry, so sometimes I suggested to the odd friend that I would be at the restaurant around

2:30, and if free, perhaps they might like to swing by for a coffee or glass of wine. I was always intrigued to learn their initial impression of my lunch companion and, indeed, how my interviewee responded to a sudden interloper into a private conversation!

Rejection and How to Handle It

I accepted that some people would not preorder my book. I have no problem with that as long as they are kind enough to inform me, but I do have a problem with desultory responses. Three stood out for all the wrong reasons. One fellow lambasted me for the rudeness of one of my earlier missives. It was sent to around fifteen hundred people, yet nobody else commented thus. Our original communication was via LinkedIn, where I responded to a few posts he initiated, and then I emailed him suggesting we meet for a coffee to develop the conversation. I did not hear back but continued to contribute to the odd thread thereafter. As his email address was openly displayed on his LinkedIn profile, I did not think it inappropriate to get in touch about my book. I explained the background, but he was full of righteous indignation that I had sent him an unsolicited invitation.

Moreover, he told me that I should "learn some modern manners." I thought manners were timeless and stated that, as a matter of simple courtesy, I anticipated he would at least revert back to decline the invitation if the book was not for him. And I enquired as to which modern manners he was displaying through his silence. He curtly informed me that if I expected him to reply to a random message, our conversation would be going no further. He clearly needed a dose of the OFFLINE formula of randomness and serendipity. What did his actions say about the way of the world?

The vast majority of addressees do not respond to an initial online enquiry, especially if it is sent as a blind copy. Whenever I host an OFFLINE dinner, I invite roughly five times as many people as I can accommodate, and I send rolling reminders. I applied the same approach to preorders for the book and enquired of those dragging their feet if they were hiding under the duvet. Lucky I was so polite! Yet he took umbrage in the most surprising fashion, hence our rather short and sharp exchange.

I reflected further upon it and concluded it would be worth another bash to see if we could find common ground. I emailed him again, stating that when I was a young man, I had been advised by a wise old bird that you should read a newspaper whose views appeared diametrically opposed to your own one day a week and you may find you don't disagree with them quite as much as you thought! Perhaps he might like to join me in that spirit and let us see what we might learn from each other. As yet, I await a response. I suspect it may never arrive.

I invited another associate to preorder. Again, I followed up, as she did not bother to respond. She had a bit of form in that regard. She had not replied to any prior invitations to the OFFLINE dinner. I understand people lead busy lives, but very few are so frantic that they cannot take a minute to send a brief email. I met her at an event hosted by a mutual connection, and I learned too that she had worked with one of my sisters, which she had much enjoyed. All seemed fair and lovely in the garden. Might I be honoured by a response? Indirectly, yes. Her automated email response advised that she was attending a world-class programme in high-performance training to help her become the best person she could be and create an unforgettable life.

I suggested she ought to try out my training schedule, which involved watching football while eating all the pastries, a different kind of discipline. She acknowledged my note, and then all fell silent again. I followed up on both my invitations to buy the book and attend the dinner. This finally drew a riposte. She was not enjoying an apparent barrage of sales messages. I was simply seeking the courtesy of a reply either way. It is not enjoyable when you carefully craft a message and recipients do not bother to revert back at all. Is that attitude representative of modern manners? I do hope not.

I am not unsympathetic to their views. There is an ongoing bombardment of messages, texts, emails and apps in all directions. However, I was surprised at how quickly they took offence at my missives. They evidently deemed their respective stances entirely justified and it reminded me how difficult it is to look at the world through the eyes of others. Additionally, innumerable individuals whom I know well failed to respond at all. I am not specifically pointing the finger at them, but this episode showed how the online universe has distorted conventional behaviour.

Compare this with the actions of my friend Tony, such a generous host when I stayed with him in Wyoming. He was quick indeed to respond to my invitation to preorder the book but told me that he was travelling through Asia on a heavy schedule and was "very busy." In fact, he was so busy he could not possibly waste a moment to support the home team. I advised him that it would take a mere five minutes to preorder while lying in the bath. Perhaps the ugly truth is that Tony is more inefficient and a poorer delegator than he would care to admit!

Predictably enough, he did not respond. People can use their time as they see fit, albeit I find it slightly tragicomic that Tony, an extremely successful man by any measure, still prioritises the pursuit of business around the globe. If I was in my seventies with the freedom to come and go as I please, I would not be inspecting factories in India or Vietnam. There are far more pleasurable things to inspect but, regardless of my personal preferences, I was slightly taken aback by how quickly Tony disregarded my request. The sale of one more book was of no material consequence, but it was more about the lack of intent.

One observes parallels in other ways. If a friend asks me to donate to a charity bike ride, for example, I will always seek to assist. It may not be a cause I particularly espouse myself, but I recognise the sacrifices made on all fronts and try to do the right thing. As I do with Big Issue sellers on the street, who are homeless and working to build some kind of permanence for their future. It is vital to demonstrate a generosity of spirit, yet it is astonishing to witness how many members of the public walk past the vendors as though they were invisible.

How Much Is Enough?

Alas, this conduct is representative of an increasingly selfish world where maximum personal reward seems inextricably linked with minimum personal inconvenience. There is nothing wrong with striving for success and financial comfort through the capitalist system, but there are more meaningful symbols than the mere accumulation of assets. Has there been a behavioural shift since coronavirus? More screen time, less human contact and no sense of proportion have all contributed.

After the first lockdown was lifted in London in late 2020 and before the next one was imposed, I went for a walk along the river Thames with an old friend and neighbour. It was a crisp, bright, rather serene day, and as James and I strolled through the park, one could readily forget that a global pandemic was wreaking havoc in every direction. It was a moment to reflect on what was most important and life affirming to me. As the waves gently lapped against the foreshore, you might call it a watershed moment.

I said to James that I could see him and that he could hear me; we could fortunately get around unaided and had control over our respective diaries while we each had a roof over our heads and could put food on the table. What else really mattered? How much, how often, what colour, who cares? The natural resources of our planet are becoming fearfully depleted by the frenzy of humans taking what they want from it, not what they need. There is a quasi-addiction to consumption. How many shoes would truly enhance my wardrobe options and transform my life? Last time I looked, I only had one pair of feet!

From Ship to Shore

As I mentioned earlier, I rarely find myself at a business conference all day. On one particular occasion, though, I had a meeting mid afternoon and thought I would stick around to listen to the key-note speaker. He was talking about security, which did not conspicuously appeal, but I took a gamble. If the speech proved rather dull, I could always slip discreetly out the back door, yet I stayed for the duration and I was extremely pleased that I did so.

The speaker was a fellow named Alan West, or, to give him his due, Baron West of Spithead. He had previously been first sea lord, the most senior serving position in the Royal Navy, and his distinguished career included action in both Iraq and the Falkland Islands conflict. Upon retirement, he was in high demand from organisations in both the public and private sectors seeking to benefit from his outstanding leadership skills. One role he accepted in 2007 from the government was to help devise the National Security Strategy, the first integrated review conducted in the UK on the threat posed by terrorism, cybercrime and biological and chemical warfare. A heavyweight committee, embracing prominent figures in business, public service and the government itself, was formed to consider ramifications of the strategy and an agenda was sent in advance of the inaugural meeting.

Alan West stated that the committee meeting was due to start at 9:00 sharp, so he arrived himself around 8:30 to collect his thoughts, have a cup of tea and chat briefly beforehand with members of the committee. Yet he sat there alone until 8:50, whereupon he asked his secretary to lock the door and turn off all phones if nobody had shown up by 8:55. She protested that she could not voluntarily block such luminaries from the meeting, but West told her it was an order and she duly complied! At three minutes before the hour, they heard footsteps outside, and someone attempted to open the door. A couple more people appeared, and they could hear muffled and agitated voices and the fruitless ping of messages. Was it the wrong room? Was it the wrong day? By 9:00, there was a small throng of committee members in the corridor, joined by latecomers, but they all filtered off by about 9:10. West asked the secretary to unlock the door, reconnect the phones, sit down and take the minutes of the meeting. The minutes recorded the fact that he was in the chair at the appointed hour, but none of the committee had turned up on time, and, therefore, the meeting had been annulled. And the minutes were dispatched forthwith in that unredacted form.

He explained that when he was commander of a ship with five thousand crew members, he routinely made it his business, if not in the heat of battle, to give them his time, whether junior officers or the regular company, and to recognise their contributions. It might have been a private word of encouragement or guidance on a technical matter or perhaps to enquire about the family of the sailor and the performance of his football team. It was a simple matter of courtesy on his part to acknowledge that everyone was playing a vital role. The committee, however, had shown a dereliction of duty through sloppy timekeeping and should be called to account.

As it was the first time they convened, he anticipated the committee would at least be punctual. Occasionally, there may be genuine reasons for lateness, but to have received no messages or calls from them or their assistants or colleagues advising him was unacceptable. He stated that it is almost impossible to attend a meeting of that magnitude and hit the ground running. You don't just flick a switch to shine a light. Their lack of mindfulness and respect for the committee they sat on was startling to West, but his actions certainly had the desired effect. They were never late again. Indeed, he said, they fought to be first!

Mind Your Manners

Standards are slipping everywhere. The former Health Secretary Jeremy Hunt was called out by the Speaker for using his mobile phone during a debate on bursaries for nurses. Perhaps he was enraptured by the local election results. Perhaps he was making a doctor's appointment. Perhaps he was playing *Candy Crush*. At least he was thoughtful enough to turn down the volume.

The Speaker is known to be fastidious about upholding matters of procedure in the House of Commons. However, he does not limit himself to affairs of state. In April 2014, I was returning by train from Liverpool. I had watched Arsenal lose 3–0 at Everton, a game in which we were comprehensively outplayed and had just sought the relative comfort of a seat as I mused over the defensive frailties of my team. My friends took a pair of seats across the aisle, and I took the only available space opposite. I asked the smartly suited and booted fellow facing me if I might join him and he invited me to sit down.

I momentarily closed my eyes in the sanctuary of the seat. When I opened them, I realised my travelling companion was none other than the Speaker, John Bercow. I hinted that he looked a touch overdressed for a game of football, but he explained that he had been the guest of his parliamentary colleague Andy Burnham, the mayor of Manchester and a passionate Everton supporter, in the director's box. There was no explicit dress code, but as a courtesy to his hosts, he had erred on the side of caution. Jeremy Hunt, by contrast, displayed no courtesy at all.

Our conversation was engaging and stimulating, and my friends across the aisle contributed to it too. We particularly wrestled with the conflagration that is the Middle East and how the inebriated chanting at the other end of our carriage revealed so much about our society. I suggested we continue the conversation over lunch, but inexplicably, he appears to have had one or two greater priorities keeping his house in order! Our trip home was a slice of OFFLINE, a convocation of argument, thought and laughter.

One of the clear lessons from this unexpected exchange is that you should always try to look vaguely presentable. You never know who you might bump into. Moreover, there is no need to stand on ceremony with people in the public eye. They walk, talk and go to the toilet just like everyone else, but as ever, the key to great conversation is to be interested in other people and what they have to say. A little flattery can go a surprisingly long way, for if you make people feel good about themselves, they tend to return the compliment.

Yet there are frequent examples of the reverse effect. When Jennie Churchill, mother of Winston, invited the playwright George Bernard Shaw to lunch, he telegraphed, "Certainly not. What have I done to provoke such an attack on my habits?" To which she replied, "I know nothing of your habits; hope they are better than your manners." She may have inhabited a very different world than our own, but the fundamentals of life don't much change through the ages. Same scenery, different actors. Regrettably, kindness, consideration and courtesy are all too often regarded as an afterthought in the business arena today.

The cut and thrust of commerce seem to preclude the really important stuff, but good manners are not a luxury item to only be wheeled out on birthdays and anniversaries. Appreciation should be visible and meaningful. Emily Post, the renowned American expert on etiquette, pointedly stated that "manners are an awareness of the feelings of others. If you have that awareness, you have good manners, regardless of which fork you use." I very much admire the attitude of the proprietors of a café in Cordes-sur-Ciel in southwest France who routinely charged €2.60 for a coffee but reduced that to €1.80 when the request was preceded by "Please" and to €1.30 when accompanied by a cheery "Good morning."

When you acknowledge the contribution of colleagues in a genuine way, it says much about your own character. A handwritten note will certainly make its mark. Recipients may not necessarily recognise your eloquence nor, indeed, your scribbling, but it is the thought that counts! "Please" and "thank you" are two powerful calling cards. Try to use them more often and look people in the eye when you speak with them. Your counterparts, typically, will reciprocate in kind. It is a simple mark of respect to listen well, but listening and hearing are not the same.

All Talk and No Action

The concept of give and take is an accepted business maxim, but I much prefer to give and then give again. You will make yourself almost indispensable by offering to assist, introduce or facilitate without instantly expecting anything in return. Natural givers will recognise that quality in you and, typically, will follow suit. Givers don't seek to take advantage of their counterparts but instead provide a platform to build lasting and mutually beneficial relationships. Every initial meeting carries an element of speculation.

One of the greatest impediments to business success is a failure to actively pursue these connections. It may be they offer no value at that specific moment. Indeed, such connections may never yield any commercial value, but it is the personal dimension of these relationships that is most crucial. The key is to look beyond the obvious and develop a rapport. This is the glue that binds people together, although its adhesiveness depends on you!

Whenever I receive a business card, I record the details in my address book and send an email to the individual concerned. Unless there is a particular point I wish to raise, I just state that it was a pleasure to meet them and that I would be delighted to continue the conversation over a coffee. Who knows where it may take us?!

Venue is important too. I like good coffee, and I like good service. I like diversions, and I like distractions. I want to take my counterparts ever so slightly outside their comfort zone, so I am not averse to conducting an informal chat while wandering around a museum to surreptitiously glean a few clues about their personality. What reaction does the art elicit from each of them? Who may be lifted, emotionally and spiritually, by the images on display? What can I learn about my companion? Some people do not respond to my emails at all. In selected cases, if I think the connection might be valuable, I may renew contact, but often I discard them. However, I am very receptive to those who respond positively. Do I have an occasional eye for the possibility of some advantage? Perhaps. And so should you. But I will always seek to reciprocate accordingly. And so should you.

The OFFLINE philosophy embraces the virtues of an open mind and a generosity of spirit. Nobody is suggesting you become best friends or go on holiday together, but when you give naturally, you induce feelings of warmth and curiosity. Nurture those feelings and bask in their glow yourself. It feels good. You should do it more often.

Pay it forward. Next time you are queuing up for a coffee, offer to buy one for the person behind you. Why? Why not?! It is simply a good turn, and the response it draws may be positively heartwarming. For the sake of perhaps £3, you unexpectedly brighten someone's day. Who might follow your example and display similar consideration?

When I put a kiss at the end of an email, it is just an expression of warmth and concern, but it is instructive to see who embraces it and who does not. Some men seem to regard it as an affront to their masculinity. Givers are far too preoccupied spreading lovingkindness to worry about such minor quibbles. If you impart and share without fear or favour, self-imposed barriers and inhibitions start to evaporate. Givers do not carry an invisible scorecard in their heads to calculate your relative worth to them. That is the domain of the takers.

The act of giving should not be purely confined to the business environment. Givers recognise that it is often the incidentals that help cement long-term relationships. Their door never closes. The golfer Gary Player famously declared that the more he practised, the better he got. Giving may not be a natural tendency for some but, if you work on it, you will find it immensely rewarding. Every connection you make possesses its own ecosystem, so at least attend to the basics and ensure you follow up each meeting promptly, proactively and progressively!

Donald Duck Is Running for President!

I wrote this parody before the US election in 2016 when Donald Trump was still campaigning for the presidency. He was, indeed, voted into office, and sadly, he is still around today. The queen is no longer with us, which is sadder still.

The queen recently revealed, in an unguarded moment, that she believed the behaviour of the Chinese ambassador in London was rude. Quite right too. He displayed neither manners nor courtesy. I would trust her judgement on this, given she has seventy-odd years of diplomacy under her belt. Indeed, at the age of ninety, I think we can cut her a bit of slack after decades of public service. By contrast, Donald Trump deserves to be cut no slack at all after decades of strictly personal service, all designed to massage his preening ego. I don't need to go down into a coal mine to know it is dirty and dangerous and, correspondingly, I don't need to be an American citizen to recognise that Donald Trump is a vulgar, divisive man. He is professionally offensive and takes pride in diminishing, demeaning and demonising anyone who challenges his view of the world.

Bertrand Russell, the famous philosopher and polymath, remarked that man is a credulous animal and must believe in something, and in the absence of good grounds for belief, he will be satisfied with bad ones. The American populace is often alarmingly naive and gullible and will believe any old rubbish if it is delivered in convincing fashion. It is even more susceptible to the tongue of a serpent. Trump panders to a constituency that warms to his vainglorious claims that he will reassert US dominance and make the country great again. Unfortunately, he completely misses the point, which is not about America winning anything but about its contribution to creating a more secure and equitable world for the future.

Trump's expansiveness adeptly camouflages his ignorance of policy detail. There is a mighty big difference between a display of strong-arm tactics and being presidential. Arm waving and shouting are usually the preserve of traffic policemen, but perhaps that is his real level of competence. A president should reflect the will of the people in both message and conduct. I judge leaders by the way they treat the lowest common denominator, not the highest, and the queen implicitly understands this. Regardless of her personal views, she does not stamp her feet and squeal like a schoolgirl, as Trump does, nor gratuitously offend and seek unfair advantage. Should the unthinkable occur and Trump were ever elected, expect a conversation at the Court of St James along these lines:

Q: Herr Trump, Willkommen zu meinem bescheidenen heim. We are each immigrants of German descent. Isn't integration a fine thing?

T: Yes, ma'am. Our countries share so much. Marching bands, golf, grand houses. I like your place. Not quite the splendour and taste of Trump Plaza, of course, but it certainly has scale. If I may say, the silver could do with a polish. I can barely see my reflection from here!

Q: Oh, Herr Trump, you are such a card! The Chinese will be enchanted by you. Where next on your world tour?

T: France, but I hope they speak decent English and remember their place. I am, of course, the latter-day Sun King.

Q: How impertinent of them to speak their own language! How do you manage with your Mexican friends?

T: They have their uses. Indeed, I have an army of tiny Mexicans who are very close to me. They prop up my golden mane and are grateful for the job. I am truly a man of the people.

Q: Oh, Herr Trump, you extend your largesse in so many directions!

T: My largeness? Oh yes, I am big everywhere.

Planet Earth is dangerous enough without Donald Trump at the helm. Narcissism is never an attractive trait, and certainly not in a political leader. Much of the civilised world is appalled that a cartoon character could become US president. His rallies are a mixture of slapstick and tall stories with just enough intimidation to browbeat the opposition. They are utterly bereft of fact and substance and merely an excuse to rattle the electorate with his pernicious brand of scaremongering and ridicule. Who in their right mind would wish to endorse such a candidate? Apart, of course, from the frightened and the foolish and apologists for the NRA, the Ku Klux Klan and their charmless friends?

A month ago Donald Trump had never even heard of the Brexit movement, and now he is pronouncing that its success is a step towards true democracy. How very statesmanlike! What other dazzling insights can we expect from Mr T? He is pro wall, anti-Obamacare, pro marriage, anti gun control. He has no time for any questions, thank you. Don't you know he is a very powerful man? He has a business empire to run, he has many influential friends, and he is far too important to talk to you. And yet he still finds time to comb his luxuriant thatch. Captain Fantastic, vanguard of the American way of life, here to fend off the scourge of the Democrats. Don't think you can argue with him. He is the brains behind Trump University, after all. He will show you who is boss, and if you don't agree, he will sue you. Expect a US federal deficit in the trillions under his tenure as the world countersues in various guises.

There is an important distinction between political correctness and popular correctness. The former substantially reflects an establishment view of appropriate codes of conduct, whereas the latter is more concerned with an expression of public sentiment. Trump wavers between the two and has a secure footing in neither. He is much more preoccupied with burnishing his Everyman image, which should come in very handy when he sits down for a Chinese state banquet with the premier and his entourage. I do hope Trump remembers to mind his manners, especially when he discovers Peking Duck has been renamed Donald Duck. The Chinese do so admire American culture! What greater compliment could they pay? Trump, Drumpf, Schmuck, Duck—what's in a name? Not much, apparently. America needs Trump about as much as a bald man needs a barber. But the people have spoken, albeit incoherently.

Present and Incorrect

Food, Glorious Food

I can't cook. There it is, the plain, unvarnished truth. I never have and I probably never shall. And I can't say I have ever had any yearning to do so. I enjoy food in its various guises but not in the planning, preparation or cooking of it. I am a great believer in playing to your strengths, so I specialise in the eating department. Sixty-odd years of practice have not been entirely wasted, as I do have an appreciation of the efforts of others, but I have never felt I should be standing shoulder to shoulder with them in the heat of the kitchen. Cooking is a bit like skiing or driving in that they are all generally challenging to execute with any natural proficiency when you first approach them in middle age. Skiing is much more easily adopted as a child, when your body has elasticity and you have little sense of fear. Sitting behind the wheel of a car can be a daunting prospect when you are flummoxed by the technology of your vehicle, let alone the actions of the other drivers on the road. Cooking induces similar feelings in me. It is complicated enough working out which appliances and utensils I might need and how they function before I give a thought to any recipe.

It might have been different had I been encouraged to get involved as a boy. But I was never invited into the kitchen in a meaningful way. Nobody ever said to me, "Chop this, stir that, taste these." The usual refrain from my mother was "Come back in three hours or we will call you when lunch or supper is ready." She no doubt took her cue from my father, who managed to navigate his way to the fridge or larder with relative ease but never actually cooked anything. The kitchen was just a conduit to somewhere else in the house, hallowed ground where neither he nor I ever much lingered. Like father, like son, she reasoned, and she was pretty much on the money there.

Nonetheless, I was always keenly aware that sharing food acted as a binding agent. It brought people together, and it was one of the reasons behind the success of the OFFLINE dinners. On certain occasions, I would throw a broad subject like food into the wider conversation to see how everyone in the room responded. At one dinner, I shared with attendees three things I loved to eat and one I hated. The former reaffirmed my long-term love affair with the pastry counter. Custard doughnuts (with sprinkled sugar for the purists among you) sat atop the pile followed by mince pies and malt loaf, two stalwarts from my youth. Conversely, I told them that I can't bear lychees. The texture, smell and taste of them turn my stomach. Yet for others I know they are a great delicacy.

Having revealed my preferences, I invited the room to reveal their own and, indeed, their fondest memories of food. People certainly stepped up to the plate! One fellow, whom I barely knew, rhapsodised about his grandmother getting up early each day to cook him Turkish eggs for breakfast before he went to school. I am not sure what makes an egg Turkish, as opposed to Greek or German or American, but it did not much matter, as his recollection was suffused by his love and appreciation of his grandmother and her sacrifice. And that was what I most remember. He was followed by a couple of others with whom I was connected via the art world. One of them, whom I knew as an artist in London, revealed that in a previous life, she had owned an award-winning restaurant in Kuala Lumpur. Another attendee, now an art dealer but who once messed about on boats, was in fact an accomplished sailor retained to deliver yachts from one port to another on behalf of owners. He was always keen to mark the occasion appropriately and, if both time and weather conditions were on his side, he would prepare himself a full English breakfast in the galley. His fry-up would routinely include bacon, eggs, sausage, grilled tomatoes and mushrooms and I could envisage him on deck tucking in as the seabirds hovered expectantly above, awaiting his scraps.

An appreciation for food took a different twist at OFFLINE when I asked everyone at another dinner to put their hands up if they could cook. Every hand rose apart from mine, although I was spared any potential ignominy as I was asking the questions! I then asked them to keep their hands up if they reckoned they were good cooks.

That whittled the field by approximately half before I presented the coup de grâce: Keep your hand up if you think you are a great cook. Four hands remained up, so I asked them each to share their signature dish and what inspired them to create it. The dishes all sounded delicious, but I was especially taken by the concoction of Bassel, a Syrian lawyer who had rapidly fled his country due to the political regime and reinvented himself as a torchbearer of its culture through music and food. Indeed, his description of chicken with pomegranates and almonds, tinged with the memory and smell of home, was quite an emotional experience for him and for us too. It spoke of a primal desire of that which we most cherish, the warmth of strangers, the intimacy of friends, the nourishment of body and soul, the very essence of OFFLINE at its core. After the four of them had regaled us with the intricacies and pleasures of their respective dishes, I told them I would be coming around to their place for dinner to experience these signature dishes for myself. And as a brief postscript, I hoped they had enough chairs as I suspected that plenty of others in the room would want to join me there.

I am not particularly dazzled by the state of the table, the cutlery or the way the napkins may be folded. These special effects do not enhance the occasion for me in any way. Nor am I enthused about the concept of a tasting menu, where one is offered minuscule portions and the joy of their design should amply compensate one's empty stomach. Call me a philistine, but when I sit down, I want to eat. I do not wish to be called to prayer at the crucial moment, nor do I wish to hear a blow-by-blow account as to how each course has arrived in front of me. Yet the latter is a fate that befalls me annually when I take Frederique out on her birthday. She is French and far more sophisticated than I so her vision of culinary heaven is the polar opposite of mine. Last year, I had the dubious pleasure of accompanying her to the restaurant of Hélène Darroze, a stellar Parisienne chef, now based in London. It was located next door to the Connaught Hotel, a byword for elegance and a venue with which we forged an extraordinary and serendipitous connection just a couple of weeks later.

As for the lunch, I thought it would never end. Course after course arrived, none of which I can now remember, but I cannot readily forget the maître looming over us as each course appeared. He felt compelled to share the journey of everything from field to table, so I had to listen to a wondrous tale of a cabbage plucked from the foothills of the Himalayas, transported by a yak covered in a ceremonial robe by some ancient forager. Or how the truffles had been picked from a single patch in the Italian countryside under a full moon. I think he was trying for some kind of spiritual effect here, but it was wasted on me. At one stage I was inclined to tell Frederique and the maître that I was just popping out for a bite to eat around the corner, as he would probably still be talking by the time I got back! I resisted the temptation, and dishes then emerged with rather greater frequency to sate my hunger. However, the most important thing was that Frederique loved the entire experience, and as I mentioned in a prior context, there is a pleasure in sharing the pleasure of other people, even if it does not necessarily accord with your own. In fact, the highlight for me was when we were guided around the kitchen downstairs after lunch, an area so commodious it comprised the kitchens for both Hélène Darroze and the Connaught side by side. I had never seen so many people in white hats before! But the French have always possessed a deep appreciation for fine cuisine, which reminds me of a wonderful cartoon depicting two young children at the supper table, an American boy and a French girl. The boy asks the girl if her family say prayers before they eat, to which the girl retorts, "No, we're French. We know how to cook!"

Shortly afterwards, we embarked on a two-month trip to South America. Travel is our one major indulgence and, after the coronavirus shackles had been finally broken, we wanted to make up for lost time. We selectively explored Argentina, Brazil and Uruguay. One diversion took us to Boipeba, a little island off the coast of Bahia in Brazil, where we rented a house for five days. It was a charming, understated part of the world and suitably difficult to reach. A ferry from Salvador was followed by a two-hour taxi ride and a further ninety minutes by speedboat before we waded ashore. The owner of the house was very helpful and offered a number of tips about the property itself and its surroundings. He strongly recommended we visit a restaurant at the end of the beach run by his friend Andre, whom he complimented as a personable guy and excellent cook with reasonable English too. So mid afternoon one day, we wandered over there to be greeted by Andre. There was no menu. He just said he was grilling steak and to get comfortable. It would be a bit of a stretch to call it a restaurant. Upturned logs doubled up as chairs and tables, but it was delightfully ramshackle and inviting. When I went to the bathroom at the end of the garden, I saw nervous blue crabs scuttling back into their holes. We learned later that the blue crab population had become very depleted during the coronavirus outbreak. The relative isolation of Boipeba meant few supplies reached the island, so the people literally lived off the land. The blue crab was always a delicacy and was not nearly so abundant now.

Lunch was served with a minimum of fuss. Andre presented us with steak, chips and a tomato salad. He refilled our glasses, placed an incense burner to ward off the insects and left us to it. I can safely say it was one of the most succulent meals I have ever eaten. The temperature, the seasoning and the cut of beef were all sublime and they were all enhanced by the unaffected setting. You travel halfway around the world and out of nowhere, you find cooking of this quality. After we had finished, Andre sidled over and asked us where we were from. When we mentioned London, he told us he had been there himself. "In which district do you live?" he asked. We said Greenwich, and Andre said, "I know that. I used to visit there myself on my way to Lewisham Market." Frederique and I were stunned. It was surprising enough that Andre had left his island home for a long trip to the UK, but the vast majority of tourists confine themselves to the usual destinations such as Buckingham Palace, Houses of Parliament, Tate Modern, or the London Eye. Greenwich is a historically rich area with the finest baroque architecture in the land, but it is south of the river and slightly off the beaten track. Greenwich Palace, the birthplace of King Henry VIII, was in fact the precursor to Buckingham Palace before the court moved upstream in the seventeenth century.

Set beside the river, Greenwich possesses a fascinating ecosystem that could certainly have drawn in Andre, but what on earth was he doing in Lewisham Market? It is well known for its size and variety, especially its Asian and African wares. Andre went there to source interesting and unusual ingredients or spices for his job. "How long were you in London?" I asked. "Three years!" No wonder he spoke decent English! "And what were you doing there?" It seemed faintly unbelievable sitting on the upturned logs digesting lunch, and it seems faintly unbelievable right now, but Andre had been a chef at the Connaught Hotel. No wonder he could cook like a dream in his little makeshift kitchen! I love this story, as it is an embodiment of so much of the OFFLINE philosophy, but my fondest memory of that afternoon was the procession of young children who walked through his gate after school to enjoy his homemade ice cream. The sheer pleasure of that little treat, cool and refreshing, while they played and chatted with their friends and siblings on and around the logs, was a further reminder to me that small things can make such a big difference.

There is only one other meal that can match lunch with Andre in its purity, simplicity and sense of surprise. In 1986, I spent time in Bali en route to Australia. When I arrived in Kuta, which was the major town, the locals were literally dancing in the street. The reason for their excitement was that the authorities had just installed the first set of traffic lights on the island! I don't imagine they had more than thirty miles of paved roads across the island at that juncture, but, nonetheless, the erection of these lights was symbolic of their progress and entry into the developing world. Yet I also remember thinking to myself that this is the beginning of the end of Bali as a true island paradise. As tourism and technology inevitably grow, something of the native spirit dies with it. Although it remains a very desirable destination, I hark back to my trip and wonder where in the world I may next experience it.

But my most vivid and lasting memory of that detour to Bali was a lunch for ten in the north of the island overlooking the verdant valleys of Ubud. This area is home to both an artists' colony and a monkey forest, so there is plenty to attract the eye, but nothing attracted us more than the aroma from a roadside shack we randomly alighted upon. We sat down with a few beers to enjoy the superb views while a flow of dishes started appearing. I have no idea what exactly we ate, but I remember it was uniformly delicious and served with great kindness and charm. It was a fabulous mélange of flavours and sensations, and when we settled up, one of our number said it was $10. We each handed over a bill while remarking upon the outstanding value it offered when he stated it was actually $10 for everybody. It was literally a dollar a head. Now that is the kind of tasting menu I like! Once again the OFFLINE mantra of displaying an open mind and a generosity of spirit brought unexpected reward.

Animal Magic

Mynah

I must confess that my television consumption has sharply declined over recent years. I have never watched a box set, never subscribed to Netflix and have no idea about any forthcoming blockbusters. In fact, aside from watching football and the odd documentary, the only topic that consistently grips me is nature programmes. I can remember being astounded by the sheer sweep and majesty of *Life on Earth*, narrated by the incomparable Sir David Attenborough, the doyen of this genre and as watchable today in his nineties as he was in his pomp. He stands shoulder to shoulder with Fred Rogers and Dale Carnegie, each leviathans in their respective fields.

I have never owned a pet of my own hitherto and I do not have any strong desire to do so in the future. But my love and appreciation for the animal kingdom knows no bounds and few things absorb me as much. We all think we are terribly clever and sophisticated as humans but every species possesses its own toolkit to negotiate the vagaries of life. How could I forget that hyperactive mynah bird who so mesmerised me at the Amsterdam Zoo? It took me OFFLINE every which way. I had walked to the zoo one fine but frosty morning and, seeking immediate respite from the cold, I entered one of the bird enclosures where I was entranced by a very excitable mynah bird doing everything in his power to attract the attention of his mate.

He flew hither and thither, swooping high and swooping low. He danced, he sang, he brought her a morsel of food but she remained unmoved. Perhaps she was pregnant or hormonal or perhaps that slug for breakfast was giving her indigestion. So he sat on a different branch, played it a bit coy and ignored her, tweeting to himself. And then another aerial display to remind her of his charms and remind himself that he was a bird. He cosied up to her again, nuzzling and nudging, but to no avail. So he started tidying up the apartment, rearranging the furniture and sprucing himself up but he clearly needed guidance from the bower bird, surely the Picasso of the bird world, which creates extraordinarily complex and artistic displays to attract a female. Watching the frantic activity of this mynah certainly warmed me up, if not the outside temperature. His vocal range and solicitousness to his mate were both commendable but he was a bird of modest appearance, lacking the plumage of some of his more exotic avian cousins.

Toucan

The infinite variety of birds has been a source of wonder to me from the moment as a young boy I saw a drawing of a quetzal, a fantastically bright and colourful little creature, which is the only animal I know that has lent its name to a currency, as it is both the national symbol of Guatemala and the face of its banknotes. I have never entered a store in the US and handed over fifty bald eagles or a hundred bison to pay for dinner! Central and South America each host an extraordinary array of wildlife but it is the birds that take centre stage. There are more individual species in this region than anywhere else in the world and I had an unforgettable encounter in Colombia, where I came literally face to face with one of its most recognisable constituents.

The biodiversity of Colombia is so rich that it contains over eighteen hundred different bird species alone, most of which are only known to dedicated ornithologists, but one of them is unmissable. While I was in Cartagena, I had lunch at the Sofitel Hotel, a refashioned seventeenth-century convent whose large courtyard in the cloisters was the home of a keel-billed toucan. It had been reared as an orphaned chick by the owners and was given the freedom of the place, where it freely mingled with guests. There is an ugly beauty to a toucan, with its bug eyes and outsized fluorescent bill, but it is my kind of bird.

Although it had grown comfortable with the presence of people, we were under no illusions from the staff that, despite its relative tameness, it was a wild animal at heart and one should not take any liberties with that beak! I was quietly minding my own business over lunch when I was suddenly confronted by this toucan perching on the back of the adjacent chair looking keenly in my direction. Actually, my chips were the main attraction rather than myself but I resisted the temptation to offer him any. We spent a few minutes eyeing each other up before he flew off to introduce himself to other guests but it was a magical OFFLINE moment that took me way outside my comfort zone.

Moose

I have been unexpectedly confronted up close and personal by big beasts too. A few years ago, I was invited by my friend Tony to stay with him at his home in the foothills of the Grand Teton Range in Wyoming. This was a part of the world with which I was wholly unfamiliar and its appeal was further enhanced by its proximity to Yellowstone, one of the jewels in the crown in the pantheon of American national parks. This is a park on the grand scale, so vast that one can enter it via three different states. It was a mere sixty miles away, a walk to the shops by US standards, and, as Tony kindly allowed me to borrow one of his cars, I could not resist the temptation to explore it properly and decided to stay overnight.

The only drawback was the long delays caused by road maintenance within the park, which could not be implemented in winter when conditions are so inhospitable, but it was a fabulous experience overall. Aside from observing the Old Faithful geyser in action, I saw bears, wolves, eagles and plenty of bison, although the sheer size of Yellowstone meant I only gained a glimpse of its riches. But that was just the warm-up act for what was to follow. As Tony was in Wyoming infrequently, he employed a housekeeper to look after the property and she was extremely knowledgeable about the local flora and fauna. I had spotted a deer on the road previously and mentioned that if she saw another one or some chipmunks gambolling in the grass, perhaps she would let me know. One morning she hurried over to me with her finger over her lips and beckoned me to come quickly. Like a furtive trespasser, I tiptoed behind her into the garden, as daintily as my size-ten feet would allow, and there, alongside the low wall, stood a moose. Only one thought crossed my mind. Oh my God, it's enormous! If you have never eyeballed a moose yourself, I can tell you it is a big, ungainly creature. It stamped its feet and sniffed the air but the housekeeper told me there was no cause for alarm as it was just picking up our scent.

Her confidence was only mildly reassuring to me but she then tapped me on my shoulder and pointed to the undergrowth to our left. I crouched down trying to look dead keen, keeping one very careful eye on the moose, but I could not see a damned thing. But then I became aware of a faint rustling amidst the foliage and a few moments later a baby moose tentatively emerged from the bushes in a very spindly, wibbly-wobbly fashion. As I was clocking this, another calf emerged and they unsteadily inched over to what was clearly a mummy moose, nestling alongside her hind legs. The housekeeper whispered to me that she knew exactly when they were born. They were just six weeks old and, once the mother was comfortable that we were no threat to her babies, she would teach them which leaves to eat and how to strip them from the bark.

As she did so, I stood there transfixed like a small boy with my mouth hanging open, thinking to myself that this is truly nature in action. This awkward, hulking bovine was so tender and gentle with her progeny. I remained utterly still and silent, completely absorbed as they went about their business. A few minutes later, the mother suddenly turned towards the pasture at the front of the house with her moosettes following like a couple of drunken sailors. I beetled back inside to watch them at closer quarters but soon they descended down the valley to make a few more house calls and the moment passed, but what a truly OFFLINE moment!

Elephant

However, this was nothing compared to my experience in Botswana. It had long been a dream of mine to go on a safari and I decided that, if I was to only do so once in my life, I must make it count. Consequently, I split our itinerary between the scrub of Nxai Pan on the fringe of the Kalahari Desert and the Okavango Delta, an immensely lush, overgrown set of tributaries teeming with colour and life. We initially flew to Nxai Pan via the southern frontier town of Maun from where we squeezed into a teeny-tiny plane stacked with crates of chilis and avocados and just enough room for me, Frederique and the pilot! Flying low, we were greeted by the sight of herds of elephants crossing the plain but we got close, very close to others in due course. We were extremely fortunate to observe a troop of a dozen family members sauntering past us on one memorable drive but the most extraordinary interaction occurred in the fading light as we returned to the camp at dusk one evening.

The customised vehicles were handled with great dexterity by the guides over the rutted terrain but sometimes we moved quite slowly and on one occasion we were confronted by a bull elephant in our path. It is difficult to adequately convey just how monumental an animal it was but we let it pass in its own time. The sheer bulk of it was impressive enough and we sat there completely absorbed by this lord of his domain. As we did so, nightfall rapidly beckoned and, once the elephant disappeared into the bushes, our guide restarted the engine and inched forward. We were all slightly lulled by the effects of a day that had started at dawn and what we had just witnessed so we did not anticipate any more surprises.

This was evidently a mistake as, without any warning, this elephant suddenly trumpeted. Bear in mind that not only was it quite unexpected but it was dark, it was behind us and it was unbelievably loud! I literally jumped out of my skin but it was the most exhilarating feeling to be quite so close to the power and force of nature. It took me OFFLINE every which way and, although we were surrounded by a profusion of wonderful creatures in both locations from iridescent frogs to lazing lions, it was the elephants that took centre stage, even wandering across the air strip just as we prepared to leave the desert for the delta.

Duck

There is arguably no finer insight into the nature of the human condition than personal relationships, as demonstrated by a very devoted couple, Manny and Esther, who, despite the usual challenges of married life, enjoyed a happy and robust union. Sadly, however, the passage of time eventually caught up with them and Manny passed away. Esther got on with her life as best she could but often hankered after her late husband and, after consulting a couple of friends, plucked up the courage one day to visit a spirit medium to see if she could connect with Manny via the other side.

She found herself sitting in a darkened room, curtains drawn, as the medium started incanting over her bowl. Five minutes elapsed when Esther became aware of a noticeable shiver around her and then a plume of smoke above. As the mist gradually dispersed, she saw to her astonishment Manny's beaming face. And the conversation went something like this:

E: My God, Manny, is that really you?!

M: Sure it is, Esther! How are you doing?

E: Never mind about me. Tell me, what's it like up there?

M: Sweetheart, it's absolutely fantastic! The weather is marvellous, as you might expect in heaven, so the first thing I do every day is go for a swim. When I finally get out of the water, I sit down, dry off, have some breakfast, enjoy the sunshine and then I make love. Again and again! Then I am back in the water for another dip, cool down, catch up with some new friends, swim up and down. Out of the water, dry off, admire the view, make love one more time and then it's lunch.

E: Manny, Manny, Manny, hang on a second! Down on earth, you weren't too keen a swimmer and, come to think of it, sex wasn't your strong point either.

M: Esther, you don't understand. Down on earth, I wasn't a duck!

Observing

One can learn many lessons from poker players and their ability to read faces as much as cards, best elucidated by Al Alvarez in *The Biggest Game in Town*. His seminal account of the 1981 World Poker Championship is far less preoccupied with the intricacies of strategy than the visual cues with which players sought to take advantage of their opponents.

Yet the inability of many people in everyday life to look you in the eye, shake your hand properly or embrace you is alarming. Are they half asleep? How has it come to this? A mere twitch of recognition often encourages drivers to thank you back when you acknowledge their consideration in stopping at a zebra crossing. It is a backhanded compliment of the worst kind. Perhaps any vestige of appreciation is such a rarity that it becomes a knee-jerk reaction.

Listening

One should always listen without prejudice and, moreover, listen actively, not passively. The latter applies when you are already thinking about formulating your response and are not giving due priority to the present conversation. Fred Rogers stated that you are present whenever you listen and respond thoughtfully.

When you meet someone for the first time, don't say "What is your name?" and "What do you do?" These are pat and lazy questions. A much better method of engagement is "My name is X. What are you passionate about?" You will instantly elevate your conversation to another level as you are effectively inviting your counterpart to take centre stage while offering hooks on which to hang your hat.

Ian Duncan Smith is a Tory politician who led his party during a brief interregnum in the 1990s. Its fortunes were at a low ebb and he tellingly observed that one of the reasons for its unpopularity was that everyone associated it with what the party hated rather than what it loved. Be positive. If you are consumed by negative thoughts or only seek to disparage the opposition, your card is marked and it is very hard to break that cycle. Benjamin Franklin, the distinguished writer, scientist and diplomat, expressed this in forthright fashion by stating that "tart words make no friends; a spoonful of honey will catch more flies than a gallon of vinegar."

Stay in touch with your emotions. I am almost always reduced to tears by a wonderful video produced by Bank Sabadell of an impromptu outdoor concert on a Spanish square. The rendition of Beethoven's *Ode to Joy* is especially affecting when you watch the response of passersby completely captivated by the music and song suddenly in their midst. As they gather around a soloist, other members of the orchestra wend their way through the crowd, comporting instruments of varying shapes and sizes.

The spontaneity of the moment, the mood of anticipation and the sense of togetherness on view in this Spanish square warm my heart every time. But it positively bursts when the camera trains upon a young girl, no more than six or seven, climbing up a lamppost to obtain a better vantage point and is then so enraptured by the spectacle that she clasps her hand over her mouth and then proceeds to mimic the conductor. When your attention is so absorbed by music or words, you listen with more refinement and care.

Dancing

I was born with an unusual condition called two left feet. When I hit the dance floor, any sense of timing or rhythm is entirely coincidental, but like my performance on the tennis court, this in no way detracts from my pleasure. And dancing is a pleasure and a release, whatever your standard, perhaps best captured by the phenomenon of flash mobbing, whereby apparently random individuals come together to dance in a public space. Two of the finest examples I have seen were those at Antwerp Central Station, which in the midst of the morning rush hour, suddenly piped out numbers from *Grease* and *The Sound of Music* to the amazement of commuters.

A group of professional dancers slipped out unobtrusively from the shadows to set the tone, encouraging the crowd to follow their routines, and I was delighted to observe plenty of left feet on display! Nobody was bothered if some participants stepped to an altogether different beat as long as they embraced the moment. It was a true kaleidoscope of colour, movement and unfettered joy that literally stopped people in their tracks and epitomised the spirit of OFFLINE.

There was a similar exuberance at a huge gathering on an icy Moscow bridge, dancing to "Putting on the Ritz." Everybody was consumed by the music, the positive energy and the pleasure of sharing the moment, whatever their level. The world at large needs a bit more of the unparalleled joy that flash mobbing exudes. But I am no less tempted to watch the undoubted stars of the screen. The rendition of "Shake a Tail Feather" in *The Blues Brothers* is just the kind of street party I would sign up to in a heartbeat, and I am simply mesmerised by the foot-tapping genius of Fred Astaire and Rita Hayworth.

How often we reflect upon the folly of our youth. Now I have reached the foothills of upper middle age, I have belatedly developed a real appreciation for the music of the 1960s and 1970s. It is most unlikely I shall ever grow an Afro or be adorned by those wide lapels and lime green suits, but the music takes me back to a golden era when people got dressed to go on stage and really looked the part. The harmonies and musical tonality of the artistes were not in dispute, but the best of all for me were the dance moves, especially from a fabulous twelve-piece band called the Trammps. If ever I feel a little blue, I stick on "Disco Inferno," one of their signature tunes, and all is well with the world.

Look Up, Wake Up, Shape Up

There is no such thing as bad weather, merely inappropriate dress. Some people welcome bad weather, whatever they are wearing. Thieves and housebreakers love the rain. When it is pouring, everybody rushes around with heads bowed. Nobody looks up and thinks, oh, what a charming view. This plays to the advantage of the robber. Too many people fail to look up or down in life generally. There is a kind of tunnel vision and the digital obsession does not help. Be aware of your surroundings.

One organisation that has imaginatively facilitated such awareness is Street Wisdom, which arose from the recognition that the
simple act of walking and observing helped people reclaim their
senses. It has spawned a burgeoning interest in the life of neighbour-
hoods whereby local volunteers act as guides for groups of up to a
dozen. A three-hour stroll is an invitation to share conversation and
exercise with fellow walkers while learning more about the history of
the area.

Sometimes the group may split up for an hour and individuals are left to explore on their own before reconvening for a coffee.
Whether you spent the time wandering the backstreets or admiring
front gardens or reading memorials on park benches, it encouraged
mindfulness. There are shades of OFFLINE, as there is no objective
other than sharing the experience with like-minded people. Given
the isolation and separateness imposed by lockdown, the impact of
Street Wisdom is even more meaningful and an initiative to be wel-
comed with open arms.

In a different context, during a hiatus in the initial coronavirus
outbreak, I hosted a few OFFLINE lunches for eight at an excellent café near my apartment. These were often populated by good
friends, but, given the circumstances, I was open to anyone who was
around and wanted a human connection. The subsequent feedback
from each participant was warm and positive, except for one who did
not respond at all. We had never met before, but she was a friend of a
friend, a management consultant and a mother of two, so I presumed
she had mastered the basics of communication. Yet she sheepishly
admitted to our mutual friend that she did not know how to reply
after the event when all that was required was a simple acknowledgement to her lunch companions. There was no scary monster waiting
to trip her up, so what was she so fearful about? She had contributed
freely to the conversation over lunch, despite her initial diffidence,
yet as she convinced herself she did not know how to appropriately
end it, she decided to opt out altogether. Not so wise. I just hope she
remembers to look up when it starts to rain!

Smiling and Laughing

We were all born with a remarkable gift. It does not require ten years of study or mastery of three foreign languages. We display it naturally, and it exudes warmth and goodwill. It is a powerful emotional tool, yet we exercise it far too infrequently. It is the gift of smiling, which is a bit like leaning into a conversation. It shows interest in your counterparts. You can smile without having the faintest clue about the subject matter, not dissimilar to watching people laugh without understanding the punchline, which is so infectious that you feel compelled to start laughing too.

Laughter is a cousin of smiling. One OFFLINE attendee was neither especially clever, handsome, successful nor witty, but he had one asset that outstripped virtually every other person in the room. He had a wonderful laugh that radiated pleasure and warmth. Few possess this gift. There are occasions when you may observe a group laughing together. You may be on the periphery but the sensation of warmth and togetherness and fun unwittingly draws you in.

Thinking Time, or the Art of Doing Nothing

Many years ago, I worked with a very clever computer programmer. Aside from his command of coding and the vagaries of technology, the cleverest thing he ever did was insist on working a four-day week. It was written into his contract. So I asked him, "What do you do every Friday?" "Thinking time," he said. "I take my dogs for a long walk, and I enjoy the fresh air. I mull over issues affecting the business; I try to achieve a bit of clarity and space in my life and after lunch, I may jot down a few notes in my book. When that is all done, I often pop down to collect my kids from school. Their chatter reminds me not to take myself so seriously. I always find days devoted to 'thinking time' are so much more productive than I expected!"

Working a shorter week is not in itself so unusual. When I was growing up, I remember my father routinely was out of the office on Fridays. He was available to handle the cares of business, as required, but much of his day was devoted to charitable interests and exploring more intellectual pursuits. There might be phone calls and the odd meeting to attend but there was no sense of an agenda or diary for the day. Was he any less productive despite his apparent inactivity? Not at all. The pace and direction just adopted a different rhythm. Serious thought requires serious time. Endlessly rushing around trying to look busy is not recommended. Purpose does not always require action.

Historically, if a farmer wanted to understand and appreciate the weather better and its impact on his crops, he would put on his hat and coat and walk three or four miles to his neighbour; en route he would no doubt observe the lay of the land, the movement of animals and clouds, the way the wind blew. When he arrived at his destination, he might sit on the verandah sharing a glass of lemonade with his neighbour. They would discuss their travails and expectations, after which he would don his hat and coat and walk back home with much to contemplate. No plan other than to look and learn and perhaps change his mind. Superficially, he may have idled through part of his day, but I think he had just the right idea.

Pay Attention!

A cowboy is captured by American Indians in the Wild West. They carry their prize back to their village and prepare to scalp him as part of a festive ritual. Upon arrival, they proceed to dig a pit to put him in ahead of the celebrations. The medicine man begins his chanting, the dancers limber up, the crescendo rises and soon the cowboy is buried up to his neck in the pit. As the chief starts proclaiming the order of play, the cowboy enquires if he might make a request. The chief is a decent sort of fellow and accedes, whereupon the cowboy beckons his horse over. It bends down, and the cowboy whispers in its ear; the horse rears up, turns around and charges off. Meantime, the drumbeat grows steadily louder, the dancing more feverish, the temperature hotter and hotter. An hour passes, then two, then three. The cowboy watches on with increasing despair, but just as he is about to give up all hope, he hears the sound of hooves in the distance and the promise of salvation from his predicament.

As he flicks the sweat from his eyes, he can see his horse galloping towards him and, upon his horse, there is a beautiful, voluptuous and naked woman. The American Indians respectfully stand back, the drum beat temporarily halts, the singing quiets, and as the horse approaches, the woman dismounts in front of the cowboy. She proceeds to stand astride his face, swaying this way and that, moaning and writhing herself into a frenzy until, completely satiated, she falls to the ground in a crumpled heap. The American Indians start chanting again and crowd in on the stricken cowboy. He observes the chief sharpening his knife, the blade glinting in the sun, and knows the denouement is fast approaching. He can barely get the words out of his mouth, but with all his remaining strength, he blurts out to his steed, "You fucking idiot! I said bring me a big posse!" This is a lesson in learning to listen properly. It is so important to ensure you both pick up and deliver the right message.

I witnessed some comical, albeit less dramatic, examples of miscommunication myself at OFFLINE. The most memorable concerned a lady of a certain vintage slightly in awe of her surroundings who found herself among a throng of people when she first arrived. As I was at close quarters, I introduced her to a few guests, including my friend Johannes, whereupon she deftly curtsied in front of him, impressively regained her balance and replied, "Good evening, Your Highness!" Johannes accepted this compliment with suitable Swiss phlegm and did not allow his newly conferred royal status to limit his enjoyment of the evening.

It's All in the Stars

Fate often lends a hand in unexpected fashion. When I hosted the sole OFFLINE cocktail party, I asked all attendees to provide their birthdays ahead of the event. Some people stated their date of birth, which was not required at all, but it was quite revealing in its own way, as they were often rather younger or older than I realised! My purpose was to observe how the laws of attraction are often determined by kismet or providence. I wrote the star sign relevant to each birthday on a Post-it sticker. Halfway through the evening, I shared a few bon mots with the assembled and then called them out individually to receive a sticker.

The entire constellation was represented with a clutch of Scorpios here, a group of Libras there, a preponderance of Capricorns and a mere pair of Sagittarians. Once stickers had been applied to their lapels, I instructed them to find all those in the room who shared their star sign. The amazing thing about it was the number of people with the same sign who had naturally gravitated towards one another earlier in the evening without any awareness of their astral connection.

Nevertheless, when you ordinarily eliminate badges or designations, you force people to pay attention, as that sense of the unknown creates an element of doubt. Can you afford to overlook individuals when there is no signpost indicating where the conversation might lead you? People are often far too quick to apply a label to themselves and to others, but this is an error of judgement. Your antennae should always be sensitive to your surroundings.

What Children Teach Us

MBA Students from Japan and China

I read a fascinating article about a professor at a university on the West Coast of America. He ran the MBA programme there and after twenty-five years of tenure, he was asked about the biggest change he had noticed. He gave an interesting answer. He said that his classes in the earlier years were dominated by Japanese students. By all accounts, they did everything by the book. They arrived at lectures on time; they were diligent and industrious and appeared model students. Twenty-five years on, his classes were dominated by Chinese students, equally prompt, focused and hardworking. But there was one key difference. He stated that if he told his Japanese students that black was white, they dutifully wrote it down, underlined it and no doubt made a note in the margin. But if he told his Chinese students the same thing, they would stand up in class and say, "Professor, I don't believe you. Prove to me how black is white!"

This little parable explains why China will bestride the twenty-first century in a way that Japan could not previously. The Japanese possess more than their share of brilliance, but they are generally followers rather than leaders, certainly in the postwar generation. Any sense of preordained superiority was swept away in the aftermath of World War 2, and the Japanese Industrial Revolution during this period of reconstruction saw the people emerge as innovators and improvers, taking the ideas of others and enhancing them, whether through supply chains, management techniques or otherwise. How many uniquely Japanese inventions can you think of, as opposed to better versions of what went before? Sushi? Origami? Sumo? Each is a distinctive emblem of Japanese culture, but arguably its finest creation for the export market has been Toto, the toilet manufacturer that combines both a seat of comfort and supersonic standards of hygiene!

Party Pieces

Do you insist on staying at a party or event, however boring? I don't! Why would anyone in their right mind do that? Out of politeness? An exaggerated sense of propriety? Fear of embarrassment? Unless you are intimately connected with the host and want to fly the flag, you should always familiarise yourself with the exits, should a fast getaway be required. Why watch a disappointing film to the bitter end or plough through an interminably long or boring novel?

Conversely, there are instances where you can willingly join the party without an invitation. Since 1942, University College in London has hosted free lunchtime lectures that enable professors or other academics to share an aspect of their research with students and colleagues across all faculties and they are open to members of the public too. Some topics might be way over my head, but that does not detract from the experience as a whole. How wonderful simply to sit down with a sandwich and drink to enjoy the presence of such expertise and intellectual richness.

Another occasional practice of mine has been tagging onto the back of museum tours in the hands of a subject expert, although this can be something of a drawback when you discover, as I did a couple of times to my chagrin, that your newfound group is conversing in an altogether foreign language like Russian or Japanese! Think of it as gently gatecrashing the party, where all that matters is that you look so confident that nobody can doubt that you absolutely deserve to be there.

On the Shelf

Whenever I visit a private home, one of the first things I do is scan the bookshelves. This is an excellent opportunity to apply the OFFLINE ethos and wander off the beaten track. I can often be found secreted in the study or spare bedroom poring over a lovingly maintained set of *MAD* magazine or *Great Railway Journeys of the World*. Often the selection is a bit humdrum and uninspiring, but it does at least offer some temporary escape. Few activities are duller than traipsing around an apartment so someone can show off the size of the new fridge or the colour scheme in the downstairs bathroom.

Books have always been a pleasure to me, but I find it exceedingly difficult to buy only one book when surrounded by so many. Most people have mastered the modest art of leaving with what they came in for. I am far too distracted, even in bad bookshops. The dominant retailers are conspicuous by poor signage, predictable displays and a dearth of comfortable sofas. Yet these disadvantages are insufficient to deter me from a quick gander from time to time, if only to draw upon their breadth of stock, so imagine the state I'm in when I enter a bookshop, replete with gaps, surprises and architecturally challenged shelving. There are some quite wonderful bookshops both in London and beyond but that is another subject for another day.

I have frequently reflected on what I have bought and why. Certainly, I am conscious of how little I know about so much and one might view this accumulation of books as a natural form of education. However, it would be a misconception to consider me well read. Widely read perhaps, but well read? No. I would struggle to name five classic works of fiction that I have enjoyed. I can safely say that in adulthood, I have not granted daylight to a single page of Shakespeare, Dickens, Tolstoy or Dumas. Darkness has similarly shrouded such titans of ancient civilisation as Socrates, Plato and Cicero. The great political, economic and social tracts have been largely dispatched to forgotten shelves, and I have barely a nodding acquaintance with classical music, opera, ballet and other such cultured pursuits.

Whereas most sensible people go to a bookshop with a book or two in mind, I go to a bookshop with everything in mind, but it is precisely that sense of randomness that makes the exercise so much more interesting. And even in the worst-case scenario that nothing jumps out at me from the shelves, I have the consolation of spending time around other people who love books and sharing the experience.

What's on Your Bedside Table?

A few years ago, I was invited to a private gathering hosted by Citi Private Bank. They wheeled out various divisional heads—US CEO, global economist, the whole shebang, eight of them in a line. The presentation was interesting on a superficial level but a bit ho-hum and predictable. The moderator fielded questions from the audience at the end, all serious and worthy enquiries, but just as he was looking to wrap up proceedings ahead of drinks, I felt my arm inexorably rise at the last, as if hailing a taxi or appealing for an offside flag. He glanced over to me, eyebrows arched, so I stated that there was only one burning question for me. As I am a great believer that the world beyond informs the world within, what were the panel of experts reading at the moment? What was on their bedside table? They all looked a bit stunned, as if groping for an invisible autocue.

I didn't wait for the moderator! I simply pointed to the guy at the end and asked him the question directly. To his credit, he overcame the shock of being first in line by responding he had Dr Seuss for company as he read it to his children at night. A decent enough answer off the cuff, but it went rapidly downhill from there. The second fellow revealed he had the *Rothmans Rugby Yearbook*; the third, the Bible (I thought that kind of thing was confined to hotels in the US Midwest!); the fourth, some Grisham-esque airport schlock; number five was devouring a weighty tome about the Bolshevik revolution (and one look at him told me they were well suited); six and seven I now forget, but some salvation appeared from the final participant in his choice of Kurt Vonnegut. Ah, at last, evidence of an enquiring and imaginative mind.

At the reception afterwards, numerous guests approached me to say that my question was by some distance the most revealing of the afternoon. Business is business, but an excessive focus upon it squeezes the juice from the human dimension. Relationships and the way we engage with one another are vital, and one should never underestimate the pleasure of sharing. For the record, at that time, I was reading *You're an Animal, Viskowitz!* by Alessandro Boffa, a sublimely witty and clever book that I unreservedly recommend. It comprises a set of ironic fables in which Viskowitz assumes the persona of various animals that mimic human behaviour. So we learn of a dormouse who has erotic dreams, a police dog who is also a Buddhist, a lion in love with a gazelle, a chameleon suffering an identity crisis and many more besides.

The Same but Different

Every two or three years, a symposium is convened for all the world's leading linguists, etymologists, dictionary compilers and those generally concerned with the use and interpretation of language. At the end of their various deliberations, the delegates are given a conundrum to solve that, typically, involves taking two words that superficially look and mean the same and drawing a distinction between them. On a recent occasion, the two words in question were *complete* and *finished*, which I think you would agree do, indeed, look and mean the same. Except that one bright young spark delivered a distinction so brilliant, I think it may just stand the test of all time. And this is what he said:

When you marry the right partner, your life is complete. But when you marry the wrong partner, your life is finished. And should the right partner catch you with the wrong partner, your life is completely finished!

My Specialty Is My Generality

The actor Kenneth Williams, despite his camp and catty on-screen persona, was a cultivated and well-read man, albeit a self-confessed hypochondriac. His various ailments sent him to his general practitioner on a regular basis, but, as the years progressed, he was increasingly referred to a specialist for an expert opinion. Sometimes the specialists would recommend him to other specialists to examine one aspect of his condition. When he frothed that some doctors were becoming so granular in their focus that they would end up specialising in precisely nothing, he was speaking slightly tongue-in-cheek, but there was an underlying seriousness to his observation.

In a business or professional environment, specialisation certainly has its merits, but generalisation is much preferred, as it emphasises a curious mind. Specialisation often necessitates a deep dive into technical issues, but concentrating on your sphere of activity alone may also be viewed as very narrow and structured. Nobody is so brilliant that they can be an expert in everything and nor should they be. We each display an amalgam of skills or aptitudes, but they are not always obvious to the naked eye. In areas where we may be weak, we should reach out to those who are strong and view it as "coopertition," a portmanteau for cooperating with the competition. A clandestine attitude that rebuffs any acknowledgement of your weakness is not recommended.

Dame Nancy Rothwell is chairman of the Russell Group, which provides oversight of British universities. She advises against early specialisation at school and praises universities that give credits to students who combine arts and sciences, such as a physics student learning about Chinese culture or a literature major taking a module in neuroscience. This is sensible advice but rather states the obvious. One of the notable benefits of general knowledge is that it publicises a rounded personality and enables its owner to shimmer in multiple directions. I witnessed this most boldly during a series of quizzes I hosted at OFFLINE.

It's on the Tip of My Tongue!

In my experience, quizzes and games are unifying forces, best enjoyed in analogue form. The "Cultural Life of Cities" quiz proved a real eye-opener! The questions related to a dozen places that attendees had either lived in, knew of or had read about, such as London, Paris, Tokyo, New York and Berlin. They were designed to tease or provoke debate across each table. Which city, for example, possessed the most cinema screens or newspapers and how many? Which had the lowest carbon emissions? Or the most cycle lanes? It fuelled the most fascinating exchanges, often unravelling what people thought they knew and what they really knew! Some could not disguise their strong competitive streak and instinctively took charge of their table, pen and paper at the ready, while others participated intermittently and others barely at all. That was fine, too, as I knew the commotion in the room would unwittingly draw them in anyway.

Another quiz even more graphically exposed the ignorance of supposedly educated and intelligent people about the world around them. The "Where on Earth Are We?" quiz invited them to arrange in order the thirty-five most populous countries around the globe. I wanted to play fair, so I gave them the top triumvirate of India, China and the US with their respective numbers and presented them with an alphabetical list of the rest. In the right-hand column, I inserted all figures and invited guests to match them up accordingly. Some were completely baffled, while others rose to the occasion. They collectively appeared to redistribute a large swathe of the global population in the process, but we live and learn!

When I hosted OFFLINE for Brand South Africa, the quizzes adopted a more local flavour and related to practical issues, such as an appreciation of Afrikaans slang should you be hobnobbing with the locals. For those who wished to go native, I thought a modest command of Zulu would be a worthwhile addition to their repertoire. I shared half a dozen expressions and invited attendees to match each of them with the correct translation. Examples included *Umnumzana uzokhokha konke.* "This gentleman will pay for everything." *Uthanda ukudansa nami?* "Would you like to dance with me?" *Ulwimi ululodwa alonelanga?* "One language is never enough." The table with the highest score was then invited to enunciate these expressions to the entire room—to the amusement of Pumela and everyone else—as any hint of vulnerability or nervousness among the assembled had long since been swept aside. Any sense of ego was always stripped bare by the OFFLINE mantra of displaying an open mind and a generosity of spirit.

What Are Teachers For?

About seven years ago, I received an email from my old school. The governors were looking to appoint a new headmaster. Although they had retained a specialist recruitment company to identify the best candidate, they sought the opinion of the alumni network to supplement their formal enquiries. My principal observation was that to best equip boys for a world that would be inevitably consumed by the use of AI, robotics and their brethren, any new leader of the organisation would need to champion the virtues of human empathy and rapport. In a machine-led world, these would be essential building blocks for a successful and fulfilling future. The technological advances would generally be advantageous, but they would lie a very distant second behind the human factor. The school did not require a scholar with an outstanding academic record—there were plenty of those among the staff already. The true value was a headmaster who implicitly understood the challenge of a fast-changing world and the impact it would have on a group of adolescent boys confronting changes of their own.

Pure scholarship for its own sake has its merits, but I believe the ability to think creatively, imaginatively and provocatively matters much more. As for the curriculum, all bets are off, since it requires wholesale modification, which is relevant to the twenty-first century. The introduction of civics would represent a very good start. Rote learning will be supplanted by AI tools anyway, so thinking cognitively, considerately and compassionately will be ever more relevant in an atomised world. The governors must have taken a passing interest in my suggestion to think differently, since, although the new incumbent possessed an academic background, she became the first headmistress to be appointed headmaster to the school in its four-hundred-year history!

The Wonder of Youth

Overcomplication tends to be confined to adults. Kids don't suffer this affliction. About twenty-five years ago, I bought a picture for a few hundred pounds. When I took it home, my four-year-old son was curious to look at it but also to know what it cost. He had recently started counting at kindergarten so the mysteries of numbers represented much cause for wonder. The picture was bigger than he was so, duly impressed by its size, he sat there trying to compute a suitable number in his head. After mulling over it for all of five seconds, he triumphantly suggested £100. No, a bit more than that. He pondered a moment and said £101?! No, keep going! £102? No, higher. £103? The reality is that he took a very linear approach within his realm of understanding. It was entirely logical. If, however, you had the same conversation with an adult, no doubt you would be factoring in whether you qualified for a discount or a special deal that weekend through your loyalty scheme. Adults often create complexity and then struggle to find their way out of it.

By contrast, children can be refreshingly uncomplicated and direct. It reminds me of a tale, oft retold and with very good reason, about a young girl at school who was both recalcitrant and inattentive. One day her teacher noticed she was very concentrated in class, hunkered down, furiously scribbling away on a piece of paper. Curious to learn what had so absorbed her, she asked the girl what she was doing. "I am drawing a picture of God," she proclaimed. "That's wonderful, sweetheart," the teacher replied, "but nobody knows what God looks like." The girl looked up quick as a flash and said, "Well, they will in a minute!"

That childhood blend of innocence and insouciance was displayed in a slightly different way in a finely wrought book by Michael Findlay entitled *The Value of Art*. Findlay is an art dealer who subsequently became global head of Christie's Impressionist and Modern Paintings and his book casts a shrewd eye on the way art is perceived, the psychology of collecting and how it makes us feel. He recounted an enchanting exchange at an exhibition of Fauve artists, such as Matisse and Braque. A friend told him that he took his eight-year-old daughter to the show and, while he was still getting his bearings there, she declared, "Daddy, I don't know what your plan is but I think I will just stand here and let the colours come to me." What a mature and emotionally aware response. She would very naturally find her groove at an OFFLINE dinner!

When we are young children, we display a purity of thought that often seems to evade us as we grow older. Yet we have so much to learn from our early steps in life. We approached them in an unfettered fashion, utterly unaware of any pitfalls that may have awaited. There was a spring to those early steps. Curiosity has that effect when it is not burdened by the fear of failure. We bounded from one new experience to the next; we touched, we smelled, we pinched, we poked, we prodded and, moreover, we started to appreciate the joy of communication. And we would give things a go without worrying if we had any competence at them and also became accustomed to guess the answer to strange or perplexing questions.

The finest demonstration of this phenomenon is a TED talk delivered by the pioneering educator Sir Ken Robinson in 2006. I believe this talk has been viewed more than any other on that platform and it is easy to see why. His fundamental thesis was that the conventional school curriculum places an excessive emphasis upon mathematics, languages and the humanities. More creative pursuits such as art, music or dance are not prioritised. And why not? Because they are not determined by absolutes. They are open to interpretation and that interpretation is clearly subjective; they do not fit neatly in a box yet stymying the curiosity and playfulness of adventurous little bodies and minds does nobody any favours. Robinson proposed not a mere reform of the educational system but a revolution. The challenge is to identify the right kind of leadership in this digital age whereby all kids have the tools to equally marry intellectual enquiry with their spiritual and creative sides. Nonconformism always presents a challenge to authority but especially so when it emanates from children. It is slapped down as an impertinence, an unwelcome desire for attention, as if it is flagrantly tilting the equilibrium and validity of the status quo.

Pablo Picasso stated that every child is born an artist and that one of the hurdles we face as we grow older is to retain that artistic sensibility. Experimentation, flair and innovation are far too frequently coached out of us when young, as historically, unless you were a child prodigy, public educational systems determined that such endeavours were merely a hobby or weekend pursuit and not a pathway to a meaningful or productive career. It takes a brave, perhaps foolhardy teacher to announce that the chemistry lesson has been scrapped one morning in favour of dancing or watching a musical. It was Robinson's contention that encouraging such activities outside the usual curriculum brings confidence to children that don't naturally fit within the mainstream. And are their skills any less valuable than those of A+ students? No, of course not. A conventional education brings many advantages but not quite as many as you might think. In an automated world, thinking inside the box will matter less than thinking out of it. When the machinery takes over conventional human functions, the capacity to think and act creatively and imaginatively will take centre stage. Reading and writing, as with adding and subtracting, will remain vital skills but their relative usefulness will plateau compared with the natural freedom of expression lying dormant within so many people. The fear of ridicule, the fear of failure, the fear of stigma and the fear of the unknown all discourage us but the power of our creativity should be unleashed. Where are the future leaders to drive and inspire these changes and rattle the cage of establishment forces in the educational sector and beyond? Probably having their afternoon nap so they can recharge and recalibrate themselves to tackle the societal challenges they will be inheriting from us.

Robinson shared a personal anecdote concerning a good friend, Dame Gillian Lynne, when they were both trustees of the Royal Ballet. Over lunch one day he enquired of her start in life and she told him that she had been a distracted child, unable to concentrate in class, disruptive and forgetful. Her school hinted to her parents that she might have a learning disorder and that a specialist in that field might offer some guidance. Gillian was accompanied to an appointment by her mother who explained the background. The doctor listened attentively to them both, posed a few questions and then asked Gillian to wait alone in his consulting room while he spoke to her mother privately outside. On his way out, he turned on his radio and Gillian instinctively started dancing to the music. After chatting for a few minutes in the corridor, the doctor invited her mother to look through the window in his office. He informed her that Gillian wasn't sick at all but that she was a dancer. He recommended she be sent to a dance school, where she flourished. She said that when she arrived she was surrounded by youngsters like herself, fidgeting, tapping, twirling and moving. It was marvellous, almost revelatory to her, full of people who could not sit still and needed to move to think. There are parallels with artists who cannot be inanimate, whether changing their position, closing their eyes, pacing the room, or feeling the texture and mood of their creations. Gillian Lynne won a place at the Royal Ballet and subsequently formed her own dance company before she was introduced to Andrew Lloyd Webber. He recognised her outstanding choreographic talent and appointed her artistic director of *Cats* and *Phantom of the Opera*, each of which have received global acclaim. She enjoyed an immensely rich and rewarding career for a child once considered to be suffering a learning disorder. As Robinson pointedly stated, another specialist could have prescribed her some pills and told her to pull herself together. One perceptive and sensitive doctor set her on her way, but how sloppily she might have been pigeonholed by others who lacked the foresight to look beyond the obvious. I wonder just how many more talented, individualistic kids slipped through the cracks over the decades and were told in no uncertain terms to stick to declining French verbs or the intricacies of algebra if they wanted to lead a successful life.

Regrettably, Sir Ken Robinson passed away in 2020, a grave loss to humankind. His wit, wisdom and humanity, allied to his fervent belief in the creative capacity of children as a force for good, marked him out as a man of vision and an outstanding communicator. I feel sure he would have afforded himself a chuckle and knowing wink at the answers to the brief quiz below:

- How do you put a giraffe in the fridge? You open the door, put the giraffe inside and close the door. This tests whether you have a tendency to overcomplicate simple tasks.

- How do you put an elephant in the fridge? You open the door, take the giraffe out, put the elephant in and close the door. This tests whether you understand the consequences of your actions.

- The Lion King invites all the animals to attend a conference. One does not attend. Which animal? The elephant. You just put him in the fridge. This tests your memory.

- You must cross a crocodile-infested river without a boat. How do you make it? You swim across. All the crocodiles are at the animal conference. This tests whether you learn from your mistakes.

Roughly 90 per cent of management consultants got all four answers wrong while some preschoolers got one or two right, comprehensively disproving the idea that most executives have the brains of a four-year-old!

Technology — a Blessing and a Curse

Social Media, Ironically, Is Deeply Antisocial

One of the drawbacks of social media is that their rating systems are far too binary. Like or dislike? How about quite like? Liked you more last time. Love you but you have a couple of undesirable habits. Conversation is so much more nuanced than any online exchange, as it even allows for body language and tone of voice. It is certainly possible to live comfortably without recourse to these social media networks, but the dependency on digital platforms of most of the population renders conventional communication more difficult.

This is not a new phenomenon. In the 1930s, writer T. S. Eliot observed that people were distracted from distraction by distraction. And then the only major personal technology was the telephone! Constant online communication is exacerbating loneliness, isolation, anxiety, fear of failure, peer group pressure and a need for conformity. There is ample evidence that people are scared of causing offence, acting inappropriately, or being ostracised, marginalised or excluded. Fortunately, adopting the OFFLINE ethos strips away the exaggerated sense of propriety that stops them from being themselves.

Moreover, social media is largely a solitary pursuit. It is not as if you sit in a room with thirty-five other people, communicating via text, email, photo sharing, waving, shouting or laughing together. On the contrary, you engage in it in isolation, whether you are in the bath, on the toilet, on the train. You do it on your own and there is nothing very social about that.

A related problem is the sheer extent of misinformation, conspiracy theories and downright ignorance that proliferates online. Some 150 years ago, Mark Twain was right on the button when he stated that a lie is halfway around the world before the truth has put its shoes on. Read newspapers in hard copy, not online. Hard copy is finite, whereas online never ends; there is always one more link to follow and frequently it will take you in an adverse direction.

The Challenge of Spending a Day Disconnected

Think of the freedom of a day without mobile access. It is rare that your phone might be a lifesaver or have some crucial role to play. How did we cope thirty-odd years ago? Rather well, as it happens. Personal technology is an adjunct to our lives, not a replacement for all that preceded it. Looking at a screen late at night does more than damage your eyes. Read a book. You will sleep much better without the memory of flashing lights seared in your mind. It is shocking to see adults meet for supper and then incessantly scroll through their mobile devices. It is even worse when they do so in front of their children. What kind of example is that?

What is the ultimate test of modern times? Competing in triathlons? Conferring with brainiacs? Global fundraising? Rebuilding cities? Running countries? All mere trifles. Could you meet the mobile challenge? Spend an entire weekend without it? In the city, not marooned in the countryside where there is no decent signal much of the time anyway. Could you do it again? Consecutive weekends? A real digital detox. The world will no doubt be holding its breath. The emergence of organisations such as Summerland Camps and Unplugged in recent years amplifies the need for people to physically remove themselves from online temptations. They are akin to retreats to wean people off their digital addictions.

Esports and Video Games

How can esports be seriously regarded in the same category as physical activities? Since when have you seen chess at the Olympics? Sport involves exertion. Snooker and darts should not apply either. Nor really should motor racing, where you are basically driving around inside a spring-loaded computer. You might have to react quickly, but you spend the entire race sitting squarely on your backside.

The fact that esports have assumed such status says much about the bankruptcy of everyday lives. I see adults on the tube moving squares around a screen. Is that a game? Does this improve their cognitive skills? It is as if people want something to do to avoid entering into another world and engaging with another or with the silence around them. There is a vacuum in their lives whereby their own company is not enough. The pleasures of rumination and quiet are a bridge too far for some. Such online activity is a bit like talking to yourself. It's a kind of gentle madness.

Another gripe of mine within this sphere is the obsession with competition rather than participation. There are a number of positive video games with a significant following, such as *Minecraft*, *Farmville* and *Among Us*, a digital version of *Cluedo* improbably set on a spaceship, but anything depicting or glorifying violence or chaos gains an automatic black mark from me. *Grand Theft Auto* or *Call of Duty* are a modern-day manifestation of a trend that Fred Rogers railed against fifty years ago. There is no pie throwing but a chance instead to bludgeon your opponent into submission and storm the battlefield. Do you win any points for averting conflict in the game through nimble negotiating skills or diplomacy? Only if you are a bit soft.

Gaming certainly has the capacity to impact society positively if its creative forces apply a little more imagination and daring. The recent reinterpretation of Ms Marvel is a promising step, as Kamala Khan, its new Muslim character, embodies the spirit of the original but speaks to new and hitherto overlooked audiences. She is portrayed in this series of video games as a young Pakistani American woman, so her character addresses many contemporary issues around the convergence of different cultures, the challenges of integration and the demolition of stereotypes. Yet I feel this should just be the warm-up act. The gaming universe should be concentrating resources on other big beasts in the room, such as the desalination of the oceans, combatting coronavirus or social injustice. Gaming has created its own lingua franca, unconfined by the regular barriers of language and communication. There should be an emphasis upon its sophisticated visualisation techniques and how they might be translated into real-world solutions. How might gamers be rewarded for their efforts outside their immediate ecosystem? Perhaps an annual prize that recognises the shifting sands of technology and its applications and invites collaboration between disparate people to find common ground.

Blast from the Past

Some thirty years ago, I visited an antique dealer to try to sell a subscription to a data business that aggregated all lots from forthcoming auctions. The principals were both huffy and disinterested and told me firmly that they did not believe in technology, so I took them at their word. It was a gloomy winter afternoon, and the lights were on, so as I approached the door on my way out, I flicked the switch and the gallery was suddenly shrouded in darkness.

They indignantly marched towards me enquiring why I had done so. I merely pointed to the dimmed chandelier above and stated that the electric light was technology. As they did not embrace technology, I told them I was actually doing them a favour! I was surprised that they possessed such a narrow frame of reference. Technology permeates all our lives, often in an unnoticed, pedestrian way and many of its applications are actually very beneficial. However, social media is rarely one of them as it is one of a few examples of negtech (negative technology).

I welcome advances in technology. They are the lifeblood of every economy, whether embryonic or fully developed, but some manifestations swing both ways. Social media is one; nuclear power is arguably another. On the plus side, the application of medicine has been hugely enhanced, as has travel safety, but pride of place must surely go to flight booking systems. We would quite literally be grounded without them. The microwave is another useful piece of kit, as is the power shower and let us hear it too for the humble pencil sharpener. Don't ignore the small guys!

In a different context, it was also very enlightening attending the Goodwood Revival, which celebrates style and innovation in fashion, design, product development and retailing in the UK in the aftermath of World War 2. It underlined a latent passion, occasionally a craving, for the simplicity of the preconnected world. There was more than a hint of nostalgia, but the staging was less about the accoutrements of the era and more about the value system that prevailed in the 1940s/'50s/'60s, which has been discarded by many as an inconvenience and anachronism in the new millennium. The downside of the event was that it also showcased racing cars from the 1930s onwards that tore around the circuit, generating the most frightful racket.

Silence Is Sometimes Golden

Many years ago, my car developed an electrical fault that required the garage to dismember part of the wiring. The problem was satisfactorily resolved with one small downside. The radio and CD player were deprogrammed and I was obliged to contact the manufacturer to obtain the instructions to reset them. Alas, my technological naivety advertised itself in glorious technicolour and the procedure proved quite beyond me. There was, however, a thrillingly simple solution. Drive without them. Yet some people were rendered speechless that I could undertake a short journey, let alone a long one, without recourse to musical accompaniment. I was equally speechless that they could not.

I can't say that I felt especially disadvantaged. I was left with my own thoughts and enjoyed plenty of peace and quiet in the car but, more importantly, I observed more of my surroundings and concentrated more carefully on the road. But the good times could not last forever. They rarely do. When I bought a new car, my kids all insisted that the entertainment facilities be upgraded accordingly. My sparkling wit and repartee were apparently no match for the fabulous soundtracks to *The Blues Brothers* or *Rain Man*, nor could I compete with anything by The Beach Boys or Elvis Presley. My repertoire was thus largely confined to humming badly out of tune, reminding all concerned that I am a paid-up exponent of the charms of imperfection!

How to Be Remembered

OWSA (OFFLINE Wooden Spoon Award)

This award is traditionally given to the slowest respondents to an OFFLINE dinner invitation or to incompetence displayed in other ways. How reassuring to learn there are people out there every bit as useless as yourself in certain areas. One senior executive was so impossible to reach that his correspondent presented him with an award for the most difficult person to contact. That certainly caught the attention of the executive, who admired his chutzpah and granted him a meeting forthwith. Be persistent, use a little imagination, and you may well be rewarded.

One can swiftly achieve fame, prominence or, indeed, notoriety in the public eye, but it is remarkable just how often individuals of note can be misremembered, unremembered or plain forgotten. Even the well informed and worldly can demonstrate their ignorance in this respect. My friend Robert, one of the cleverest people I know, picked up an OWSA after a spectacular failure to recognise a notable dinner companion. Towards the end of the evening, he wandered over to another table and began an engaging and wide-ranging conversation with an elderly, avuncular fellow sitting there. He looked vaguely familiar, yet Robert could not place him. They did not touch upon their careers at all but, as they parted, Robert asked him about his profession. He replied that he dabbled in politics. This enigmatic response encouraged Robert to collect the scattered place cards from the table from which he deduced that this gentleman was none other than Jim Callaghan, former British prime minister!

In a more contemporary context, I displayed a startling ignorance of popular culture. I have been a season ticket holder for many years at Arsenal, where I have always attended games with a group of friends. Over a season we all tend to miss a few matches when holidays, business or illness has interfered with our commitment to the cause, but it is rare indeed when we miss a major fixture and Andy missed a big one. When I saw him next, I asked what caused him to skip it. He told me that he had travelled to LA for a mixing session. Something about Travis. The roar of the crowd drowned most of his words, so I just nodded sagely without the slightest clue as to what he was talking about. Andy is a very successful music producer who built and sold two record labels, but it is a world that has largely passed me by. Was Travis a person, a band, a place? The following week, I asked a web developer at my company who was a part-time DJ and knew his stuff. Have you heard of Travis? He looked at me as though I was stupid and he was probably not far off the mark. Travis was, indeed, a band and already had an album achieve platinum status, which underlines their huge global following. So a well-deserved OWSA on my part. As it happens, I subsequently met the lead singer and songwriter of Travis, Fran Healy, when Andy brought him to an Arsenal match and he was delightful company. Fran was warm, open and thoroughly unpretentious and I vividly remember him chatting about the pleasures of drawing with my son Rube, who was no more than seven or eight at the time. Fran had studied at Glasgow School of Art before forming the group and I think Rube was as enchanted by their exchange as events on the field of play. I still couldn't tell you a single song by Travis, but I can tell you that their evident blend of talent, creativity and emotional maturity burned brightly through Fran.

However, these two mishaps pale by comparison with a failure of epic proportions on my part. Truly an OWSA for the ages. I spent a few days with my friend Chad on his farm outside Knoxville in Tennessee, an area on the cusp of north and south in more ways than one. The museum there was expanding its exhibition programme and, given my connections in the art world, Chad thought there might be value in exploring a range of possibilities. Nothing ultimately came of those conversations, but the OFFLINE mantra of embracing the unexpected delivered once again. While I was in town, we were invited to a garden party at the home of Steve and Ann, both generous patrons of the museum. Steve is a very loquacious southerner involved in the lumber business who is also passionate about American football.

At that time, a series of exhibition matches between the leading teams were being played in London to raise the profile of the NFL there and Steve revealed he would shortly be flying over with a bunch of friends and fellow supporters for a long weekend to watch their team in action. Would I care to join them? As a bare minimum, I thought it would be fun to spend time with aficionados of a sport I knew little about, so I readily agreed. Just another example of accidental networking. By way of reciprocity, I invited Steve and half a dozen of his friends to join Frederique and me for lunch at the Savile Club the day before the match. They were all excited to watch their team in action at a completely new venue, so the conversation was laced with anticipation. Yet there were one or two surprises just around the corner for me too.

When Steve told me he and his gang were coming to watch their team, I learned that this was actually shorthand for the team that they owned! His wife's family had recently acquired the Cleveland Browns franchise and were busily reshaping it on and off the field. The winds of change were swirling above. On the day of the game, they picked us up near our home en route to Twickenham, headquarters of English rugby and a fitting venue for the occasion, having commandeered a coach to transport them all. When we stepped on board, it was packed, so we took a couple of seats towards the back. Amidst the hubbub and chatter all around, I noticed a couple of people behind us unobtrusively playing cards on a small table and, when we disembarked at the stadium, I ambled in apparent slow motion at the rear of the group and was overtaken by one of the card players, an old Black fellow who skittered past me. We were escorted up to their box for lunch, a generous and expansive affair, and then escorted down again to meet the players, press and sundry officials on the sidelines. But it was a blur of colour and noise and bitterly cold, so I did not linger. The sanctuary of the box and a cup of tea proved an irresistible attraction, so the start of the game rather passed me by.

The exhortations of the crowd roused me enough to take a perch outside alongside the aforementioned Black man, who was wrapped up in blankets, looking like an African potentate gazing upon his flock. During a break in play, I asked him if he was enjoying the game. He looked straight ahead and tersely said to me, "I enjoy winning." A short conversation indeed! In the third quarter, I wandered back in his direction and he was far chirpier and more animated. We chatted

about the game and his impressions of London, although, periodically and mystifyingly, spectators would clamber over barriers to greet
him in the most effusive terms. I just thought, "They are Americans,
and they do have a tendency to be rather gushing and oversolicitous
anyway." Anyhow, the game eventually finished, Cleveland victorious,
so everyone retired inside the box for warmth and sustenance and to
analyse the performance of the team in microscopic detail. I did not
sense that my insights and grasp of the tactical nuances would be in
high demand, so we thanked our gracious hosts and slipped out into
the night. As I headed for the door, I asked Steve, "By the way, who is
that old Black dude with whom I spent the afternoon chatting?" He
breezily replied, "Oh, that's Jim Brown," as if it was the most obvious
thing in the world. Only one thought coursed through my mind
on our way home: Who the fuck is Jim Brown?!

Mike is a man of Minnesota and, despite being happily ensconced
with his family in the English countryside, his passion for the NFL
remains unabated. He is a close friend of mine, and he knew I had
been invited to the game. "So how was it?" he enquired. "Loud," I
said. "With complicated rules. Endless stoppages. And the entire
coaching staff from both sides seemed to descend onto the playing
field to line up every positional move. It seemed to drag on and on.
If I had known it would be such a drawn-out affair, I would have
brought a newspaper." I told Mike that the most uplifting part of
the afternoon for me was nattering to an old Black gentleman in our
touring party. The only problem was frequent interruptions from the
crowd, as they kept appearing, clasping his hands, muttering unintel-
ligibly and looking at him with a strange kind of reverence. Nobody
swooned at my feet. I had no idea what the fuss was all about. I said to
Mike I know nothing about him except that his name was Jim Brown.

There are very few occasions when I have seen Mike completely
lose the power of speech, but he did so now. When he recovered his
composure, he gave me a steely glare. "Have you never heard of Jim
Brown? *The* Jim Brown?" I was even more nonplussed. Was he an astro-
naut perhaps, a deep-sea explorer, a writer of distinction, a captain of
industry? "No," said Mike, "Jim Brown is an NFL icon; he is American
sporting royalty. And you spent most of the afternoon sitting next to
him quite unaware of his presence and extraordinary backstory." So I
learned in pretty short order that Jim Brown had won three successive

Super Bowls in the 1960s and achieved more touchdowns and covered more running yards than virtually every competitor in his path. At the height of his footballing prowess, he retired to become an actor, starring in a bunch of B movies opposite Raquel Welch, among others, and then immersed himself in the Black and civil rights movement.

Suitably chastened, I looked up Jim Brown on YouTube. There was endless footage but the one clip that particularly caught my eye was a television interview to commemorate his seventy-fifth birthday. It brought together a group of outstanding running backs of more recent vintage to pay their respects and acknowledge his genius, one of whom, Walter Payton, by all accounts a brilliant player himself, literally worshipped the ground he walked on. It was a very touching tribute and yet the fame and reach of Jim Brown in and out of the NFL did not permeate much beyond America. Our awareness of people and places can often be cocooned by the constraints of our own environment and I am sometimes equally aghast at the failure of others to recognise the leviathans within my own world.

FOMO? No, LOMO!

FOMO sounds like a children's beverage or board game but actually reflects something rather more sinister, the fear of missing out. This affliction tends to be most prevalent among young adults who feel that, unless they are invited to or at least are aware of social gatherings, they have fallen off the treadmill of life and lost all relevance. Just left with your mobile device for company? Oh dear. Happily, I don't suffer from this problem, as I am a devotee of LOMO, or the love of missing out. Nowhere to go this weekend? Marvellous! Nobody popping over? Even better! Good company is always welcome, but not on a permanent basis. How about sleeping for longer? Turning your phone off? Going for a walk? Watching comedy classics? Is there any better way to lift your spirits? And, of course, laughter always soothes the soul.

My personal favourites include any episodes of *Porridge* and *Open All Hours*, each featuring the incomparable Ronnie Barker, and, while I am always open to fresh voices, it has been difficult to match some of the giants of yesteryear. Peter Ustinov is surely a contender for the greatest raconteur of modern times while Barry Humphries was another comedic genius I loved to watch, especially via his alter ego, Dame Edna Everage, but I am always extravagantly entertained by the kings of observational comedy, such as Dave Allen, George Carlin and Victor Borge. I am far too busy splitting my sides over scenes or jokes, which I have probably witnessed a hundred times before, to find the time to think about FOMO. I will be far too deeply embedded within the land of LOMO to worry about that kind of thing. Once my belly is full of laughter, I like a change of pace, so it is time to stick on some football highlights. This means I can simultaneously leaf through my books and return to the action whenever I hear the commentary growing more excitable and dramatic.

Lessons in Labelling

Emails are ten a penny these days, which is why they are often overlooked. However, a handwritten letter will certainly capture attention and this is especially relevant when your message is a bit more personal. If you are writing to someone at home and they wish to avoid prying eyes, sticking "Strictly Private and Confidential" in the top left corner of the envelope acts as a deterrent to others casually opening the post.

This is a bit more difficult to enforce in a corporate environment where a litany of gatekeepers and assistants might intercept said letter. The way around this is to additionally label the envelope with "To Be Opened by Addressee Only," a bit like a summons. But the ultimate weapon in your armoury is to affix a seal on the back, as nobody breaks a seal except under pain of death!

Calling Cards (Six of the Best)

Create business cards to describe individual attributes. These can be applied for both personal and professional purposes. They would display name, cell, and email, but you are effectively adding your bio in précis form. Here are some examples:

> **organiser, motivator, tolerant, eBayer, waterskier, sweet tooth**

> **green, passionate, travelled, communicator, child friendly, versatile**

good listener, gadget freak, vegetarian, tall, Francophile, shoe fetish

This is an excellent means to introduce yourself in a direct yet unthreatening fashion. It has universal application, as it offers context and an uncomplicated opportunity to start a conversation. The OFFLINE philosophy enables people to reinvent their mode of communication and unite points of interest. One might possess a few customised cards, perhaps to distribute at a business seminar or a party or to another group whose attention you wish to capture. Why have one type? Is there a rule that limits you?

Your memory of a website or email address is much more ephemeral than a sophisticated or personal card that provides both tangibility and a ring of quality. If you combine that with a great design or font, you pass on a more enduring connection. Also, when you spread goodwill and a positive message, it is much easier to take money off people. You champion your qualities and develop the concept of a courtesy card along Victorian lines. And, of course, use both sides of the card. You have paid for it after all!

Make "six of the best" a rolling feature on your card. It could represent six of the best airlines you have flown, restaurants you have eaten in, cities you enjoyed, songs you loved. Or perhaps three and three or two by three. It doesn't much matter which combination, but when you do so, you invite a client or associate into your life in a thoughtful but intriguing way. It does not diminish your professionalism but injects a whiff of humanity and personality into your communication.

It becomes a hook to hang your hat on. You could replicate the same approach on invoices to clients. That element of surprise, as you reveal something unexpected or random about yourself, could change the entire dynamic of the relationship. Also, add a photo of yourself on your card. It is much easier to build a sense of rapport with your counterpart when you literally show your face. The majority of business cards are bland, anodyne or forgettable and should be sent back to the drawing board.

Over the years, I have retained a dozen or so cards I was given. The size of the card, the imagery, the material, perhaps a particular message offer attractions. In a world more visually engaged than ever, my friend John is ahead of the game. As the former marketing director of BT, he understands the impact of first impressions. Is the rueful smile he displays on his card because he has just heard an amusing story or realised he has been a complete plonker?! A photo is so much more appealing than lines of official text.

And on a subsidiary note, why have only one version of your CV? What kind of crazy thinking is that?! Surely you want to apply a little imagination or variety to get ahead. Do you dress precisely the same way, regardless of occasion or venue? Of course not. Why should your CV be any different? Tweak it according to your audience. Moreover, your personal statement is almost always much more interesting than a laundry list of roles, which should be very much regarded as the support act when assessing the suitability of a prospective candidate.

Invoices may seem superficially dull and uninspiring, but they also provide ample scope to communicate with your clientele. The bill narrative might include, for example, (1) The pleasure of my company, (2) Time, (3) Efforts, (4) Book recommendations. The fee might be 10 per cent or 9.75 per cent and an exceptionally good lunch. Be creative: encourage a little more of your personality. The recipient will certainly remember you. Do it again. Be consistent.

Make It Personal

When you want to go the extra mile and share something more of yourself, a brief narrative to share your story can be both powerful and affecting. This is what I might say about myself, but you could adapt it for yourself as you wish:

> *Business.* **Founder and host of OFFLINE. Background in the art world. Good at reading, writing, talking, listening, interrupting and staring out of the window, though not simultaneously. Always seek to share friends, ideas, opportunities, food and whatever else crosses my path.**

> *Pleasure.* **Annual visit of parakeets to feed off the cherry blossom tree opposite my window. Second-hand bookshops. Exploring cities; Marrakech and Dubrovnik are recent highlights. Art museums and, of course, football. There is no such thing as too much football. Old street signs.**

Recommended. Anything written by Alistair Cooke. Cartagena, by common consent, the most beautifully preserved colonial city in South America. Night Safari in Singapore. London Library, arguably the finest repository of its kind in the world. Mince pies (and God knows I have eaten enough of them!).

Could do better. Airlines. Good manners and courtesy. Political leadership. Social media obsessives—it really is no way to go through life. Fruit—where are the crisp, sharp tastes of yesteryear? Why the mush that passes for mango, papaya and resembles baby food?

Virtues. Kind, inclusive, travelled, curious, full head of hair, Arsenal supporter, forthright, open-minded, excellent memory, decent taste in shoes, communicative, culturally aware. Notable ability to pack fast and light, a skill that seems to elude most people in my orbit.

Vices. I can recognisably converse in no language other than English. Tendency to look at the menu from the bottom up. Impatient. Hopelessly impractical. Utterly bereft of any musical or sporting talent. Take a good book wherever I go in case the quality of the conversation causes me to zone out.

Mistaken Identity

The final story is, indeed, very true to life, as it concerns a friend of mine, and I am sure you will be able to identify with its bittersweet nature. She is one of four girls and, sadly, their mother became steadily more infirm before starting to show signs of dementia. As you can imagine, it was difficult for all concerned, but this close-knit family rallied around, including all the grandchildren, to best care for a frail, irascible and confused matriarch. Nonetheless, there were some unexpected revelations. My friend told me she popped around to see her mother and met one of her sisters a few days later for a coffee. Naturally, her sister asked how it went, and my friend replied that she had received good news and bad. Her sister sighed and asked to hear the bad news first. My friend presented her sister with the blunt facts: "Mummy said I was an absolute cow, that I have always been the most ungrateful of the four of us, always put my career ahead of everything else and she wanted nothing more to do with me." "Gosh," her sister said, "that was bad news." So what was the good news? "The good news?! She thought I was you!" Be careful what you wish for.

Part Three

Travels of the Unexpected

Day Trip

Last Thursday brought a quite unexpected treat. Business activity was polarised by an 8 a.m. conference call and a 5 p.m. meeting and I suddenly realised that I had the perfect opportunity to wander around a museum at my leisure and, simultaneously, find sanctuary from the stifling city. New York was literally a city in heat, sweating profusely as the lank humidity enveloped it.

The subway was a revelation, however. That the station was clean and the train punctual was satisfying enough but, on stepping into the compartment, I was transported in more ways than one. The air conditioning was so cooling and so calming that I felt mildly disappointed that my rendezvous was only two stops uptown. Momentarily refreshed, I alighted and wandered in the vague direction of the museum. Having comprehensively proved to myself that I still had not mastered the city grid, I retired to an excellent café for lunch, enjoyed both sandwich and view, flirted with my book and marvelled at the sight of New Yorkers in various states of undress. I marvelled even more at the preponderance of large men walking small dogs and young men walking old women.

It was one of those rare days when there is a perfect symmetry in all one does. The subway trip was brief but invigorating, my initial walk aimless but diverting, lunch both fulfilling and illuminating. These were all themes that would be encapsulated at my destination and so it was, after getting lost again in a suitably agreeable way, I found myself standing outside that pint-sized firecracker of a museum, the Frick Collection.

I could remember very little about my last visit except that I knew I had to come again. I certainly didn't remember the sloppy customer care, epitomised by one long queue that grew ever longer until I pointed it out to the oblivious society matron ensconced at the front desk. Worse still was the surly security guard who was adamant that I could not bring my bottle of water inside but then waved me through without even a cursory frisk. Lucky nobody came armed with a penknife that day. Cultural terrorism takes many forms and I find it troubling that the custodians of such a collection could be so casual in this regard.

Once inside the main body of the building, my mood changed markedly. I was invited to take an audio guide about the collection and its contents, introduced by Samuel Sacks, the museum director, with further contributions on nominated works by resident curators and experts. And what a collection! It reminded me a little of the Uffizi in Florence whereby, almost at every turn, one confronts a masterpiece. It is, of course, minuscule by comparison but I struggled to find a mediocre picture. Certainly, there were some that I enjoyed less than others but the Old Master component was outstanding. There were a smattering of Impressionist paintings that were finely executed but this genre, on the whole, doesn't make my heart sing.

I can't honestly say I much lingered over the English portraitists either although all the usual suspects were well represented. I did appreciate, nevertheless, Frick's clear desire to seek matching pairs although the most arresting example of this was a magnificent Pietà, ironically acquired by Frick's daughter to complement a similar work he had bought earlier. It transpired that the initial one was produced by a journeyman artist as a copy of the original but it is amazing that two versions, dating from around 1460, sit side by side. That first room yielded, in my view, two of the finest works in the collection, those by Van Eyck and Memling. The former had a most luminous quality while the latter's portrait of an unknown man was compelling in its conviction and simplicity. As I moved from one room to another, I was entranced. Van Dyck, Hals, Vermeer, Rembrandt, El Greco, Titian, Veronese, Bronzino, Turner, Goya, Ingres and plenty more besides.

Frick was evidently a man of catholic taste as the house contained an abundance of furniture, sculpture, porcelain and silver. The porcelain holdings induced very different reactions, however. I found the Sevres collection, while technically excellent, almost overbearingly ornate and it drew no little comparison with the blousy qualities of Fragonard and Boucher, equally excellent in their way but which left me visibly pining for the austerity and clean lines of other periods. I prefer my romanticism a little darker.

Conversely, I thought that the Limoges enamels, housed in Frick's study, were magnificent. Shimmering as brightly as on the day of their creation, these were among the highlights for me among the decorative arts. Another notable item was a lapis lazuli occasional table, whose azure centrepiece was of the greatest precision, but it was the art reference library, looking a tad forgotten, that particularly caught my eye.

Arguably, the only disappointment about my visit is that one could gain no access to these volumes, as none were on display. How fascinating, for example, to have seen a few copies, perhaps with Frick's notes or annotations. It stretches credulity that such an immensely successful businessman, who left such an enduring legacy to the city, did not possess a significant archive relating to his art market activities. It may have been secreted elsewhere in the building but I saw no sign of it. What a wonderful opportunity to glean insights into Frick the man, in addition to Frick the collector, but it is, presently, an opportunity missed to imbue the whole experience with a more humanist dimension.

Overall, however, the Frick did the trick. The thick stone walls absorbed the heat and the collection absorbed me. My abiding memory is of a room containing El Greco's *Saint Jerome* straddled by a pair of portraits by Holbein of the two great theological rivals of the English Reformation, Sir Thomas More and Sir Thomas Cromwell. I am bound to say that the former is one of the most exceptional portraits I have ever seen—the stubble on his chin almost glistens. On the opposite wall is Bellini's *St. Francis in Ecstasy*, another seminal work, flanked by a pair of contrasting portraits by Titian. One displays a fey and sensitive youth, the other the bullish and imposing Pietro Aretino. This pair of pairs exudes ambition, intellect, power and aestheticism and it was in this room that I found the spirit of Henry Frick most prevalent.

My perfectly proportioned afternoon demanded I leave in reasonable time for my meeting. A modicum of urgency does concentrate the mind when one is so geographically challenged and I negotiated the return as serenely as the tropical conditions allowed. My meeting brought about a most interesting postscript to my day trip as, once the specifics had been attended to, the conversation turned to wider matters. On mentioning my prior excursion, my counterpart revealed that he was the personal lawyer to none other than Samuel Sacks, the museum director of the Frick. While he spoke highly of his client, he rather wearily informed me that the trustees of the museum were difficult and I had the sensation that I had witnessed a sliver of this difficulty simply trying to gain entry earlier that day. Surprising as it may seem, the paying customer does enter the equation too.

Rail Trip

I first met Dave Stevens through my friend and business partner, Mike Lee. Their relationship started most inauspiciously. Mike had been drafted in by KKR, a private equity firm of some substance, to fix an ailing investment that was shipping cash at an alarming rate. He placed a moratorium on any outgoing payments above a certain figure without his express permission. This did not sit well with Dave whose company was owed a significant six-figure sum for the supply of equipment. He doggedly phoned every hour but obtained no response. Indeed, he left so many messages that Mike's voicemail was full to bursting, thus blocking some even more urgent calls. Mike was furious and phoned Dave immediately, whereupon they engaged in a very frank exchange. The bottom line was that Mike agreed to settle the outstanding sum in instalments and they forged a mutual respect. When Mike moved to another company, he invited Dave to join his team as head of corporate sales and our paths crossed when Mike tasked him with building a presence with major US private banks on behalf of an art data business we were running.

Dave certainly announced his intentions early. While we were all in New York City, Mike and I were having a quick lunch Midtown when we received a blunt message from Dave. "Get your ass over here now. We have a meeting in half an hour with the head of American Express Private Bank." This bank had proved a tough nut to crack. AEPB was utterly wrapped up in its sense of self-importance and did not deem our upstart company worth its time. I don't know what Dave said to secure this audience at such short notice. I didn't care to ask but what I did know is that some forty-five minutes later we were sitting in the boardroom sharing our presentation with senior management. Dave memorably closed it with just four words, which have always stayed with me. "When do we begin?" compelled AEPB to respond that either they were proceeding or not and, if not, why not? I can't recall the specific outcome but I always recall the directness he displayed. As he might have eloquently put it himself, either shit or get off the pot!

Dave was a man of the Midwest down to his brown shoes. He was a native of St Louis, Missouri, where his father was a florist, and he enlisted to serve in Vietnam at the tender age of nineteen. Who knows how that experience shaped him? Dave returned home with an almost missionary zeal to live life to the full and started work as a salesman at one of the most dynamic organisations in America at the very cutting edge of technology. The company was Xerox and, wonder of wonders, they had created the photocopier. As an incentive to the sales teams, Xerox offered a highly attractive reward. The top twenty salesmen (this was the early 1970s after all!) by booked revenue would spend a week at the Playboy Mansion in Hollywood with all its attendant delights. The competition was naturally fierce but, in his first full year, Dave joined this storied group. Bearing in mind that Xerox employed thousands of salesmen across the nation, this was a considerable feat but Dave was a brilliant salesman and he certainly knew how to enjoy life!

Dave was also a creature of habit and, like many Americans, he was a man of the road. If he wasn't flying, he was driving. This presented a surprising challenge on one particular occasion, when Dave, Mike and I had travelled to Baltimore for meetings. We stayed overnight and agreed to convene for breakfast the following morning at 8:30. Dave and I kept to the rendezvous but there was no sign of Mike. At 8:45, we called his mobile but he did not pick up, nor at 9, nor at 9:15. We called his room, we knocked on his door but to no avail. His timekeeping was sometimes erratic, so we were not unduly alarmed. Perhaps he was luxuriating in a hot bath. Perhaps he had gone for a stroll around the neighbourhood. Perhaps he had genuinely overslept. Or perhaps none of the above. We were advised by the hotel reception that, in fact, Mike was not there at all. He had checked out at six without any prior warning and he had taken the rental car with him. This presented Dave and I with two problems. Where the hell had Mike gone and why? More crucially, we were due in New York City at lunchtime for another meeting with no obvious means of transportation.

Salvation appeared in a most unlikely form. The train. Not a great revelation to you and me perhaps but something of a step into the unknown for most Americans. There is no meaningful rail network across the country, although there are pockets of excellence on both coasts and on the Eastern Seaboard commuters are blessed with the Acela, a high-speed network that connects the principal business hubs. The irony of the situation is that American prosperity was built through the railways. The tracks are all there but they are largely used for freight these days, which is a terrible shame. The obsession with the automobile, allied to a desire for speed and convenience, has contributed to the diminution of community, especially in outlying areas. One of the great virtues of travelling by train is that one meets all kinds of fascinating people along the way.

Dave approached the station like a nervous teenager, as if attending a party in an unfamiliar neighbourhood. When we arrived on the concourse of the fine Beaux-Arts building, we inspected the boards to check train times. Well, I checked. Dave seemed to be temporarily paralysed, as if overwhelmed by the scale of the place and the surrounding hubbub. When I asked him which line we should take, he seemed quite perplexed. I casually enquired when he had last travelled by train. He stroked his chin, mused over my question for a moment and declared about 1965! He was decidedly out of his comfort zone but OFFLINE frequently overdelivers in unexpected ways.

We shared our table on the train with a couple of middle-aged ladies who worked for a major insurance company. The conversation was pleasant and perfunctory until we alighted upon the matter of health and lifestyle. Dave was unapologetically frank about his freewheeling habits. He drank, smoked and generally overindulged. One of the things I admired about Dave is that he lived his life without continually looking over his shoulder. Perhaps Vietnam had taught him to simply enjoy the moment rather than plan for every eventuality. The ladies were aghast. There were regular tests and checks he should be taking. How could any sensible person refuse? Did he have no sense of responsibility to himself and his family? Dave was adamant that he would do no such thing and had no desire to learn if he was suffering a potentially fatal condition. In his opinion, we could all drop dead randomly anyway so why have that spectre hang over you? Sadly, Dave is no longer with us but I have little doubt he will be manning that giant cocktail cabinet in the sky while simultaneously practising his golf swing and landing another sales contract.

Road Trip (Anfield '89)

I have been fortunate enough to attend many wonderful games following Arsenal but nothing can ever come close to Anfield '89 in terms of sheer drama and intensity. Its roots lay in Anfield '88 when Anthony and I travelled together for the first time, having been introduced via mutual friends who recognised our kindred spirit and passion for the club. Regrettably, Liverpool were such a dominant side that year that our debut appearance in the away end was inevitably overshadowed by events on the pitch.

As I recall, Liverpool won 3–0 that day and my abiding memory was of Peter Beardsley chasing a seemingly lost cause, keeping the ball in on the touchline itself, picking himself off the floor and proceeding to set up another goal. Every tackle, every attack, every move was greeted with acclaim by the Kop, a swaying, roiling mass of noise, and we were well beaten long before the referee blew the final whistle. We rounded off the afternoon by standing all the way back on the train. Were we disheartened? Not a bit of it. We decided we would apply for season tickets together there and then as we could see, despite the result, that we had the basis of a good side.

The following season certainly proved eventful. Our youthful team proved dogged and feisty but they could also play a bit. They led the table for long periods and I well remember how they were applauded off the pitch in February at Goodison by the home supporters after dispatching the hosts 3–1. Even Gus Caesar played a blinder that day. Of course, everything was overwhelmed the following month by the Hillsborough disaster and our forthcoming fixture at Anfield was postponed until the end of the season. We had obtained our tickets originally from a lawyer friend of Anthony's whose firm acted for the club and, by the grace of God, they remained valid. I cannot imagine we would have managed to obtain them otherwise, especially given the media frenzy post Hillsborough.

Liverpool did not play for a while in the aftermath of the grief that engulfed the city so Arsenal continued to accumulate points in their stead but, with the finishing line in sight, we started to stumble. Perhaps nerves kicked in for both players and supporters, given we had not won a title in eighteen years, but Liverpool remorselessly ploughed on, energised by the emotion of the city itself and the country as a whole. Our penultimate home game against Derby saw us capitulate 2–1, a defeat notable for a superlative volley by Dean Saunders for the visitors. Worse was to follow midweek as we squandered the lead against Wimbledon to draw 2–2. Liverpool, naturally, kept going and thrashed West Ham 5–1 in their game in hand to take a three-point lead into the denouement at Anfield.

Our manager, George Graham, remained confident about getting a positive result but there was a pervading sense among the fans that we had thrown away our opportunity. Liverpool were at home, they were in form and the force was with them. Anthony and I had pre-match concerns of our own. How were we going to get there? In their urgency to screen the game, ITV had not considered the pitfalls of showing it on the Friday night of a bank holiday weekend. Live football, however, was a major rarity in those days and this title showdown possessed all the right ingredients for a television audience.

The journey up proved a nightmare. Anthony drove, I entertained. Despite leaving early in the afternoon, we were confronted by shocking traffic. There were major roadworks outside Wolverhampton, allied to the usual incompetence of drivers blithely unaware there was a game on and a very important one at that. The congestion was so heavy we saw cars, vans and coaches, all festooned with Arsenal regalia, turning off the motorway to find a local pub to catch the game. We, however, would not be denied. Anthony pulled out all the stops extricating us out of the mire and flogged his MG all the way up the hard shoulder of the M62. We heard on the radio that the kick-off had been delayed by twenty minutes due to the congestion but, by the time we actually arrived at Anfield and dumped the car, the game was well underway. We ran like the clappers to the turnstiles and, miraculously, I found the one gateman still at his post. There were a couple of people ahead of us and the gateman insisted on escorting them to their seats first. We dutifully trailed after them, gaining an occasional glimpse of the action before he finally showed us to our own. We sat down, Liverpool had a shot routinely saved by Lukic and Rush limped off. Thirty minutes had elapsed. It remained goalless but the rest of the half was something of a blur. We simply needed to absorb the occasion first.

The atmosphere was electrifying. The Liverpool crowd are conspicuously animated, draped in swathes of banners and flags, an indefatigable Mersey choir, immersed in the game, the club, the city. The only comparable set of British supporters in my experience are those of Glasgow Celtic, some ten thousand of whom descended upon Highbury for a testimonial for David O'Leary on a rainy Tuesday night and sang their hearts out from start to finish. Simply magnificent. The Arsenal supporters down the far end at Anfield were energetic, if a little apprehensive. The margins were very fine. The team had to win to be level on points but required a two-goal victory to clinch the title. Liverpool's goal difference was four superior to that of Arsenal but, evidently, a two-goal defeat would square it up.

The action resumed and proved largely uneventful until the fifty-second minute. A free kick was floated into the Liverpool penalty area whereupon Alan Smith applied a deft glancing header to nudge the ball home. As he ecstatically wheeled away, the Liverpool team, almost to a man, surrounded the referee complaining that the ball had gone in directly and should be disallowed. Ronnie Whelan, the Liverpool captain, led the protests as a posse of his teammates harangued the referee. To his great credit, the referee immediately shooed away all the Liverpool players and went to consult his linesman. They stood, almost nose to nose, deep in conversation, the eyes of the world upon them. We held our breath. They conferred for maybe thirty seconds and then the referee turned sharply away and pointed to the centre circle. The goal was given. Game on!

Anfield was pulsating and crackling hot at 0–0 but, suddenly, Liverpool, supposedly invincible Liverpool, were vulnerable, a goal behind, the weight of expectation upon them, looking uncertain whether to stick or twist. At 1–0, the atmosphere rose yet another notch as the Arsenal players and fans started to believe and the Kop responded in turn to rouse their team. Chances were few and far between. With about fifteen minutes left, the underrated Kevin Richardson slipped Michael Thomas in but he rather scuffed a hurried effort and Grobbelaar saved. There was consternation aplenty at the other end as Arsenal pushed up in search of the crucial second goal and we witnessed Aldridge, Barnes and Beardsley break with Adams our only line of defence. For once, thankfully, Liverpool took the wrong option and overran the ball.

It was impossible to gauge when the game was due to end. Of course, we had a rough idea but this was before the age of fourth officials waving an electronic scoreboard around. There were numerous stoppages and delays as Liverpool knew a 1–0 defeat would be enough to secure the championship. The famous image of their midfield warrior, Steve McMahon, so graphically indicating there was only a minute left will burnish the memory of every Arsenal fan but nothing will burnish my memory quite like the move in the dying embers of an extraordinary season. Lukic bowled it out to Dixon who, in turn, pumped a long ball forward to Smith. His cushioned lay-off fell into the path of Thomas, ghosting in from deep. He took it in his stride, gained a fortunate ricochet off the defender, and was suddenly bearing in on goal.

We were at the other end of the ground and our seats were in the lower tier so it was difficult to judge the trajectory of the ball but Thomas waited and waited some more and then, just as desperate Liverpool players lunged in, he coolly jabbed the ball beyond Grobbelaar. For a nanosecond or so, time seemed to stand still until we saw utter bedlam in the away end and the Arsenal players cavorting with joy. There was one further Liverpool foray to repel but we managed it and, when the final whistle blew, Anthony and I stood there shellshocked, almost disbelieving, hugging, holding, mumbling to ourselves. We had won the title in the last minute of the last game by the tightest margin possible. We pipped Liverpool on goals scored, a just reward for our attacking football over the season. It was almost too much to take in. I vividly remember the fellow next to me saying that, despite the fact he was an Evertonian and an arch-rival, he felt sick that Arsenal had snatched victory at the last but the psyche of the city of Liverpool was such that tribal instincts were secondary to the unity created in the wake of Hillsborough. I respected that as, indeed, I respected the newsagent the following morning who stocked every newspaper on God's green Earth so we could properly drool over and celebrate accounts of that memorable Friday night.

The journey home, by contrast to the journey there, was pleasurable in every way. An Arsenal towel, draped over the car and flapping in the wind, made no secret of our allegiance as we and numerous returning supporters honked and hooted our way back to London for the real partying to begin. Yet one of my lasting memories is our late supper in Chinatown where I observed the Liverpudlian public, mournful, disappointed and emotional, recognise, despite their private heartache, that we had conquered the castle fair and square. As with ports the world over, Liverpool is a melting pot of races and peoples, a fiercely proud and partisan city but imbued, nonetheless, with warmth and good grace, sporting to the end, a place for which I retain a soft spot, regardless of events on the field of play. Liverpool was a footballing leviathan but our sweet nip of glory, delivered with such a rapier thrust, presaged a relative decline in its fortunes and I am delighted they are once again serious contenders. The name itself always brings a smile to my lips. How could I ever forget Anfield '89?!

The Power of Brands

I have a friend who has always been a very intrepid traveller and some thirty years ago he independently visited China with his wife. They were staying initially in Shanghai but, much as they were enjoying the delights of that fine city, he also wanted to check out a provincial city about six hours away by car. He was cautioned by his hosts in Shanghai about the risks of such a trip. Don't expect to find a bunch of friendly locals or university students wanting to practise their English with you. Nobody will understand a word of what you say. You may be an object of curiosity but you will largely be on your own.

My friend was undeterred. He had been around the block a few times, a loquacious Glaswegian well versed in the challenges of life. Everything was paid in advance, including hotel and transportation, with contact details to hand in the event of an emergency or random acts of God. They were advised to set off in the late afternoon, once the chaos of rush hour traffic had abated, and so began their journey into the unknown as dusk was falling.

The first two or three hours were fairly uneventful as the taxi made serene progress after escaping the clutches of Shanghai. The vista swiftly changed, however, as a diminishing urban infrastructure ushered in endless farmland. They swept along the motorway without undue alarm when the driver suddenly veered across two lanes, off the road, down the embankment and at full throttle sped through fields of corn.

My friend, understandably shocked by this dramatic turn of events, started remonstrating with the driver who, of course, spoke not a word of English and ploughed remorselessly on. As he desperately sought to calm his panic-stricken wife, my friend glanced out of the back window and saw the lights from the motorway recede ever farther into the distance.

It was now pitch black as they seemingly travelled on a road to nowhere. And then a light appeared ahead and it became clear the driver was heading in that direction. He turned sharply onto a dirt track and followed the light. A few outbuildings came into view and then a farmhouse. The car pulled up outside whereupon, without so much as a backward glance, the driver got out and strode purposefully to the front door. He knocked and he waited. No response. He knocked again and waited some more. No response. He rapped hard and the door shot open. There stood a craggy, weatherbeaten man who, after whispering conspiratorially with the driver, peered at the car and beckoned him in.

My friend sat there considering the possibilities. Even in the pale light surrounding the farmhouse, he could see his wife was mute with shock. What should he do? Make a run for it? Where would they go? The luggage was in the boot. Could he carry it off with his stricken wife over his shoulder? This was before the age of mobile ubiquity and, besides, what were the odds that he could pick up a signal while standing in a cornfield in provincial China? It is bad enough getting a signal in a cornfield in provincial Britain. And that is today!

A number of scenarios coursed through his mind but the likelihood was that either they would be discovered in a shallow grave, denuded of all their possessions, or there was an entirely plausible explanation for this unexpected detour. He only chose to share the latter option with his wife. Minutes ticked by, accompanied by mutual cursing, cussing and contemplation. And then the door to the farmhouse opened. The driver and his host exchanged courtesies while the latter peered quizzically again at the frozen figures in the car. The driver promptly clicked his heels, wheeled around and, without a hint of acknowledgement, got back in his seat, put his foot on the gas and careered through cornfields once again. A few minutes elapsed before the lights from the motorway loomed back into view and the taxi, picking up even more speed, straddled the embankment and rejoined the traffic heading to their destination.

The remainder of the journey was untroubled. They arrived in good time but another surprise awaited. The hotel claimed not to have received a deposit for the room and, consequently, there was no confirmed reservation. This is ordinarily a taxing situation but especially when you have travelled six hours into an unknown land and experienced an emotional rollercoaster en route. Nobody spoke any recognisable version of English. My friend became progressively more agitated but to no avail. A crowd started to form in the lobby of the hotel, muttering and gesticulating. No room appeared to be available and the hotel did not accept credit cards. No amount of yuan or dollars were sufficient inducement yet the answer to his predicament was literally staring him in the face.

The manager noticed my friend was wearing a Rolex watch. He inspected it carefully and broke into a wreath of smiles. The watch would provide ample surety and was a lesson, even in rural China, about the power of brands! Suddenly a room was available and all manner of creature comforts to accompany it. A quick call to the Shanghai connection the following day resolved the problem with the hotel and my friend and his wife enjoyed exploring the city thereafter.

But what, I enquired, was your off-road experience all about? He explained that there was, as he had hoped, an entirely plausible explanation for their diversion. The Chinese authorities had recently introduced toll booths to help offset the cost of the burgeoning motorway network. The taxi driver did not want to pay but he knew a friendly farmer who would let him drive across his land to avoid them. And I expect the conversation when he popped around went something like this:

"Liang Meng, come inside, put your feet up. Did you bring that bottle of Johnnie Walker for Grandma? You know she always likes a nip or two before bedtime! And those cigarettes from the big city. How was the journey over here?"

"Dong Bao, it wasn't bad at all until I took a shortcut to avoid the traffic. I turned off the road, as you do, and the fellow in the back starts ranting and raving and throwing his arms around. It was embarrassing, frankly, and terribly bad manners, especially as I was doing him such a big favour."

"I know what your driving is like, Liang Meng. Presumably your pedal hit the floor and you belted through those sheaves of corn."

"Dong Bao, he carried on shouting but I kept my composure. His wife was much more polite. She didn't say anything at all!"

"Let them relax, Liang Meng, while they enjoy the cool night air and the sound of birdsong. Fancy another bowl of noodle soup? It will give you strength for the long drive home. And strength to deal with the fellow who shouts and waves his arms."

Hospitality takes many forms. Travel can, indeed, broaden the mind but it can narrow it too. How easily we misinterpret signals and good intentions. How frequently we envisage worst-case scenarios.

Meanderings in Mexico City

This was a trip in which everything that could go right did go right. Serendipity sat on my shoulder from beginning to end. There were good days, great days, strange days and surprising days but there were no bad days.

Its genesis was an impromptu invitation from my friend Klaudia to visit her in the charming hill town of San Miguel de Allende, a roughly four-hour drive from Mexico City. We would meet intermittently in London through our mutual friends Jim and Alison; one spring evening, sitting in their kitchen, she revealed that, after many years dovetailing between New York City and London, she was returning to her roots in Mexico. Klaudia is a very warm, sociable and direct woman and she cut to the chase. What was I doing over the summer? At that precise moment, I was doing nothing and so my fate was delightfully sealed. I must come to San Miguel and I did.

The trip started to take greater shape when I recalled I had a standing invitation from my friend Tony to stay with him in Wyoming. Tony is in his early seventies, a notably shrewd, successful and urbane man with a range of global business interests who spent a month every summer in his secluded home in the shadow of the mountains outside Jackson. Wyoming was a part of the world with which I was as unfamiliar as Mexico. I knew it was in the north of the country and that it had a funny name and that the bison ran free but I'm perhaps pushing it a bit there. More importantly, I knew that Tony would be a terrific host and that I would have the freedom to explore as I saw fit. Was the invitation still open? Absolutely.

I had long been intrigued by Mexico City. Frankly, any city with a population of twenty million or thereabouts commands attention, an immense melting pot of humanity. Mexico City seemed so dominant, so dynamic and so disordered in the context of the country as a whole that I concluded that I would be completely insane to travel all the way to Mexico and not embrace its throbbing, chaotic capital. I had read mixed reports about kidnapping, drug cartels and street crime but I was not unduly perturbed. My faith was rewarded. It was fabulous. Room for improvement? Oh, yes! Cause for optimism? Even more!

Back at base camp in London, meantime, a little preparation was required. My outline plan was to fly from London to Mexico City and then make my way to San Miguel a few days later. Thereafter, I would head for Wyoming, via as yet indeterminate means, before spending the final weekend in San Francisco. My transatlantic arrangements were much the easiest to establish; everything else was a bit more complicated. But can there be such a thing as a good complication? I only pondered over this because serendipity introduced herself to me in a most unexpected way.

A presumed benefit of credit cards is that a slew of points may be exchanged for affiliated products and services. It's not the worst idea I've ever seen and many people swear by it but, regrettably, my head just isn't turned by crates of wine, gardening equipment, golf clubs or sensible weekends away. The only obvious benefit to me was the ability to redeem points for hotels and flights but the process of registration, authorisation and activation was so slow and laborious that I never had the patience to complete it. However, some two hundred thousand points couldn't be ignored indefinitely, so I took a deep breath and called American Express. I knew it was a professional and efficient organisation, but I hadn't appreciated hitherto its emphasis on customer service. They guided my faltering steps with a benevolence normally only bestowed on the very young and the very old.

The bottom line was that Amex, as my de facto project manager, set me on my way. I discovered that I could use my points tally to fly economy from London to Madrid, business from Madrid to Mexico City and first from San Francisco back to London. And to top it all, I was advised that I could combine my remaining points within a sort of cash and kind hybrid. So it was that I spent a week at the new W Hotel in Mexico City for effectively £50 per night. All material costs had been met and I had barely heard the flutter of notes.

I always travel light, accompanied by my commodious brown bag, its robust constitution belied by its mottled skin and middle age. I never overpack as, unless you are literally going to the middle of nowhere, one can always acquire supplies along the way and I like to be as unencumbered as possible. Anyhow, off I went, at a preternaturally early hour, to Heathrow, caught my connection to Madrid and thence on to Mexico City. The flight was the flight, predictable enough and vaguely on time. My first glimpse of the capital was a bit of a shock though. As we descended towards the urban sprawl, the sheer vastness—and then the flatness—of the city hit me. There are no skyscrapers in favelas.

The other thing that surprised me was the weather. Rather foolishly, I imagined I would be draped in sunshine but a proverbial hop and skip from the tropics. I actually arrived in the aftermath of a brief storm and the view from my seat was misty, bleary and wet. The drive from the airport to my hotel was uneventful, aside from a cacophony of horns, and so I finally graced the W with my presence around teatime local time. I had previously stayed at the W in the US on a couple of occasions and it was something of a departure, so to speak, from the mainstream luxury hotel brands. Sleek and chic, aspirational and confrontational, it's a bit too stylised for my taste, but, hey, for fifty big boys a night, I wasn't complaining.

This was the first foray by W outside the US and they were keen to make a splash, as did I in fairly short order. My room was spacious, comfortable, cleverly designed and ergonomically sound. It even had a hammock in the bathroom, no doubt to absorb the city with a greater sense of contemplation, alongside a fantastically complicated shower that I struggled to master. It certainly looked good, suitably primped and polished, but as I stood there naked, grappling with every button and knob, the water shot out in all directions. I must have simultaneously turned on the foot shower, power shower and regular shower plus the sprinkler system for good measure. The bathroom was drenched, let alone me, but, as I peered out and surveyed the endless city, I thought to myself that this trip, this tale of the unexpected, would lure serendipity from her lair to sit squarely on my shoulder.

Having mopped up most of the deluge, I got dressed and popped down for a bite to eat, armed with some magazines for company. The lift was slow to ascend to my floor, so I had a quick gander of my surroundings, as you do, and spotted a sign beside the exit exhorting guests to take the stairs in the event of an earthquake. Earthquake?!

I didn't see that in the guidebook, though I did recall mention of the volcano above and beyond the city, which evidently contributed much to the steamy conditions in the air and the instability under-foot. I headed straight to the restaurant downstairs but supper rather came and went for me. I was dog tired and the subdued lighting, chimed for courting couples, just about finished me off.

I awoke refreshed, if not energised. I was excited to just get up and out, a man without a plan, curious and intrigued. The hotel was located in quite a swish neighbourhood called Polanco, which I ascertained contained the greatest preponderance of synagogues in the city. As it was Saturday morning, I thought I might hook up with a few of my brethren while offering prayers for my safe arrival and a dormant volcano. The concierge helpfully pointed out a dozen synagogues on the map, the nearest of which was no more than a few hundred yards from the hotel.

This particular house of worship was actually a shteibel, a small gathering of conspicuously orthodox Jews that typically occurs in private residences rather than communal buildings. This service, however, was conducted in an annexe of a big synagogue. I don't imagine the congregation was ever of a size to fill the main hall but perhaps they just craved the intimacy of their tight and claustro-phobic world. These were frummers, paid-up members of the black-hat brigade, and I found them both fascinating and discomfiting. I think they felt similarly towards me. Once they had reassured them-selves that I was not the messiah, albeit my Arsenal T-shirt did cause an understandable moment of consternation, they relaxed and wel-comed me in. I had no idea what they were saying but I took a pew and enjoyed the view. The service rattled along with a few faintly recognisable prayers and songs. They all participated, some in highly animated fashion, some mumbling into their beards and some while in apparent slumber.

Yet my overriding thought was that this scene was a reenactment of a thousand other scenes 250 years ago on the steppes of Eastern Europe. Inward-facing communities, still a little terrified of the world around them, desperately clinging to a belief system that, some-what perversely, they share today with zealots of other persuasions. Moreover, they represented the very antithesis of Mexican manhood, scraggy, pasty, unhealthy. I truly felt an island within an island. I was invited to the kiddush, where I spoke to a few younger congregants whom I recognised from the service. They were all brothers, so consumed by their Judaism that it was difficult to imagine any life beyond. "Yes," they said, "we have been to London, to Golders Green. Do you know it?" "Yes," I replied, "I do know it. Where else did you go?" They looked at me blankly. Time to go. I thanked them for their hospitality and emerged into the street, squinting in the sunlight. I was pleased I attended the service and observed the Jewish experience through a different set of eyes but felt little or no affinity with these people who so resolutely shunned the world around them. I just don't understand that kind of blind, unquestioning faith, whatever its religious hue.

I promptly moved from one extreme to another as I stumbled across a street market just around the corner. I say stumble, as there was so much action on the ground that it was difficult to circumvent the tightly compressed stalls. Packaging, goods, animals, small children, construction of a variable nature—all crossed my path. It was loud, bustling, multicoloured and followed no obvious pattern. It was the complete reverse of the shteibel, and I loved it. I didn't linger excessively though, as I wanted to get a bit more of a feel for my immediate neighbourhood. I wandered around the side streets and saw at close quarters for the first time the extraordinary racial mix of the Mexicans, the indigenous Indians and the exogenous Europeans and more variety within than Heinz could ever wish for. I didn't dally, however, as I had a rendezvous at 2 p.m. and I wanted to quickly freshen up at the hotel.

A rendezvous? Perhaps that would be a slight exaggeration. I was meeting someone I had never met before and it was quite conceivable that it might be over before it started. When I originally planned this trip, my mother-lodes were Klaudia and Tony, in San Miguel and Jackson, respectively. I had no roots, no friends, no nothing in Mexico City but two interesting connections developed before I left London. The first was rather slender, but the second was tenuous at best. I mentioned my trip to an associate in London over lunch—indeed, somebody I didn't know especially well—who suggested I get in touch with an old friend with whom he had studied for his MBA in the US. He said that Franz was now the CFO of Coca-Cola in Mexico, which was a very big deal. Coca-Cola is revered in Mexico, rather like Marks & Spencer in the UK, a byword for solidity, respectability and a management training programme that every graduate aspires to. Anyhow,

I made a mental note and treated Sean to the lunch by way of thank-you. The second connection was so vague that I had no expectation it would yield anything at all, but serendipity was discreetly winking at me once again.

As you may have deduced by now, I am unenthused by the various social networks that have proliferated over recent times. I have no particular desire to join Facebook or Twitter and share my thoughts with a bunch of strangers. I prefer to meet real people in real life. I cannot deny that these networks do have some value and provide platforms for disparate individuals to share passions and interests, but there is no quality control. Any schmo can join and post any old rubbish. I cannot imagine why the network presumes some passing comment about a transient celebrity can grip my attention, but there it is. I do belong to a couple of networks myself, but one, LinkedIn, is substantially business orientated. Rather corporate, a bit po-faced and earnest and definitely in need of a site redesign but quite useful, nonetheless, as a stepping stone into various market segments. The linkage, moreover, is via personal referral, so you have some grasp of the value of an individual connection. The other network is a curious animal called ASmallWorld, which is only accessible by invitation but does throw up a motley selection of people and places.

This closed network essentially combines business, travel and pleasure. It is very international in scope, city centric and encompasses a broad swathe of members. I was introduced to it many years ago by my friend Ned, but I am not the most assiduous online net-worker. Some people join these platforms and, within five minutes, have 493 connections, while I, by contrast, have been on ASW for the better part of a decade and have reached the storied heights of perhaps fifteen. It's useful and diverting to browse through various listings, reviews and recommendations if only to get an idea of who and what you can safely avoid. Certainly handy if you need a good dentist in Mumbai or want to charter a yacht out of Sydney, but less so if you are not mesmerised by the prospect of a twenty-four-hour shindig in Ibiza.

I looked up the Mexico City forum and posted a brief message to the effect that I was due to visit shortly and would appreciate a few insights into the capital. Respondents were variously residents, business travellers and the like. All were helpful, but one missive stood out. It was sent to my personal mailbox on the site by a charming lady named Lillian who stated that a friend saw my message and suggested she should get in touch. Lillian declared herself a very proud Mexican and said she would be delighted to show me around the city. She had lived there a number of years, knew it intimately and was around that first weekend. I thought that was a result in itself, but it got better. Her photo revealed an attractive woman, albeit my ability to enlarge the image for closer inspection was betrayed by my technological incompetence. No matter. I asked her for her mobile and we provisionally agreed to meet at 2 p.m. on Saturday afternoon.

She turned up at the W at the appointed hour and, in suitably effusive fashion, greeted me with a hug and a kiss and told me how thrilled she was to meet. I was pretty thrilled too. Lillian was, indeed, very attractive, not too shabby at all, her Latina blood spilling in all directions, a rather intoxicating mix. We ambled over to the car whereupon she told me that she was extremely pleased to meet me and that she was taking me to San Angel for lunch: "It is very pretty, very Mexican," she says. "There is a lovely market and a bazaar. You will like it very much." San Angel is the home of many film studios and was, I suspect, once upon a time a little town in its own right, now subsumed within the outskirts of the metropolis, but right now, I was much more interested in Lillian.

She was talking nineteen to the dozen while I peered out of the window, trying to get my bearings, seeking some sense of my surroundings. I was absorbing as much as I could, but there were distractions, and one of them was Lillian, whose conversation, a bit like the traffic, veered off in all kinds of directions, sometimes without any warning. Anyhow, she was yabbling away on this and that, as I concentrated manfully on her accented English and the nature of her undergarments, when a name starts to crop up with some regularity, a fellow called Vicente Fox. And I thought to myself, "I know that name. I have seen it in the newspapers, on the web, wherever." But I was jet lagged, sidetracked and quite unable to coax my memory into gear. Luckily, my chaperone was well placed to fill me in. It transpired that Vicente Fox was president of Mexico for seven years and Lillian is his ex-wife. I had been in the country for less than twenty-four hours. Whatever next?!

Lunch was next. I was starving. Lillian, naturally, knew everywhere in San Angel and we pootled in and out of craft shops, galleries and hidden courtyards until a sharp shower sent us scurrying inside to a nearby restaurant. It was busy, so we sat upstairs to eat and talk. Rather, I ate and she talked. The food was good and the mood was good. We wandered around the market thereafter, umbrella aloft, linking arms, laughing and pointing and chatting. Could it get any better than this? I was not sure about that, until Lillian said she had put the following day aside for me too and wondered if I would like to accompany her to Teotihuacan. I had never heard of it but with all the nonchalance I could muster, I responded, "Of course, absolutely, always wanted to go there."

So it was, around noon on Sunday, that Lillian collected me from my hotel, and we drove to Teotihuacan. This proved a fascinating journey. Lillian had much to say on many things and I had the sensation that I was the perfect passenger. I was interested, a good listener and from a land far away. I observed a snaking line of shacks beside the motorway, grinding poverty all around, helpless and hopeless, shrivelled lives, a savage contrast to the affluence of Polanco. Lillian told me that people in these communities work hard, they do their best, but the machinery of state is unwilling or unprepared to invest in the infrastructure that will give them a chance to escape the scrap-heap. Ambition for most runs no further than earning enough to feed their families, avoiding the inevitable temptations of petty crime and staying alive until tomorrow, whereupon the same cycle of daily survival continues. There are parts of the city into which you just do not venture. "You must not go there," says Lillian. Even the armed police do not go without trepidation. She was very firm. I listened quietly and carefully and gazed upon the steepling mountains looming ahead on the hinterland.

I had boned up on Teotihuacan overnight in my *Time Out* guide-book. I discovered that it was a very serious number, arguably the most important archaeological site in the entire country. Mexico, lest we forget, was the home of two of the great civilisations of ancient times. The Mayan and Aztec Empires were both forces to be reckoned with, cradles of much invention and not a little bellicosity. Teotihuacan was the epicentre of this region for over six hundred years, and excavations have uncovered a city brimming with ideas and sophistication, culturally alive yet professionally managed. When they first clapped eyes upon it, the Spanish conquistadores were agog at the organisational skills required to build and maintain a multiethnic community of such complexity.

The modern history of the country is no less interesting. Lillian, of course, had been not unadjacent to the seat of power and some of her revelations were startling. They were startling for her trenchant opinions, her openness and the fact that she periodically raised her hands to make her point as we zipped down the motorway. She informed me that every pillar of state is corrupt. Police, government, judiciary, church, they are all susceptible to the coin. It is curiously covert and overt. Who really knows who controls the affairs of state and does the dirty work? I heard that a much-loved and respected friend, a senior political figure, was bumped off by an assassin on a motorbike. No clear explanation was ever given for this hit, but the anguish on her face bore its own story.

Inequality can be measured in different ways. Gun law is one means of reinforcing superiority, but so too is economic hegemony. I knew Carlos Slim had a bob or two, though I was pretty astonished to discover that roughly 85 per cent of the Mexican GDP was controlled by just thirteen families. It's the kind of thing you might expect to hear about some African kleptocracy, not a country pushing for recognition as a poster child for progressive reform. I have no doubt that Slim and his acolytes are major employers and contribute to the wider economy, but it is the density of influence that I find most alarming. Still, she brightened us both up when she stated around 15 per cent of the overall population consider themselves members of their Indigenous tribe rather than citizens of the state. One in seven people have, evidently, voted with their feet and opted out of the system.

The traffic was building up as we approached Teotihuacan. On Sunday, admission is free, so every man and his dog were on their way, plus his wife, her mother, his kids, his sister's family, whoever else could conceivably fit inside the minibus, car, truck or mode of transportation. We inched forward, and Lillian bought a bag of fruit from one of the roadside vendors. It looked like nothing I had ever eaten before, but she gave me one and proceeded to deftly peel her own. I was not quite as deft. Indeed, I displayed all the dexterity of a man wearing a pair of oven gloves, but I got there in the end, careful not to spray juice in all directions, as one is wont to do. Apparently, it was a type of cactus fruit, slightly tart but altogether delicious. We polished off a few, parked and wandered down to the entrance.

Time Out was not wrong. It was a huge site. There were temples, pyramids, burial chambers, living quarters and the like to explore. Indeed, this was only the main section. There were other structures stretching towards the horizon, some inaccessible, others subject to ongoing research and scrutiny, but there was more than enough to occupy us already. We climbed up, we climbed down, over turrets, around ditches. We admired the wall paintings, the native ingenuity, the urban planning. Naturally enough, Lillian had visited this important landmark before but only in an official capacity, as first lady. And how did it compare this time? The knowledge that I was the only security detail was a relief in and of itself. The thought of being followed around by bodyguards seems so intrusive, but I expect you get used to it.

"Was your husband particularly interested in Teotihuacan?" "No," she explained, "that was definitely not Vicente's thing." No culture vulture leading that administration, by all accounts. Evidently, he would do the necessary, shake hands, say a few words, pose for photographs and bugger off, leaving his aides to sweep up behind him. He was a man with his eye on other prizes. By another set of extraordinary coincidences, it emerged that he had risen to power through his record running Coca-Cola and set out for political life as state governor of Guanajuato, home of San Miguel de Allende, which I would soon visit.

I can but imagine how it feels to be continually in the public eye. My appearance has never been deemed a matter of national significance; I have never opened my front door to paparazzi nor had my wardrobe dissected. Nobody seems very preoccupied with my hair, my highlights or my fringe. I have not endured endless state ceremonies with people I do not know and do not much care for. Yet there are clearly a few perks—private jets, exclusive invitations, fawning courtiers, the usual trappings of high office and, of course, never suffering the indignity and hopelessness of flagging a taxi in a crashing storm. How was she adjusting to her new life? Pretty well, it seemed. Happily divorced, she had her own place, worked in real estate selling everything from prime residential to hunting lodges, was close to her four children and was simply enjoying her freedom. Her former

husband was quite a controlling man who had restricted her movements and activities outside official circles, so there was a refreshing
spontaneity to Lillian, a captivating hint of girlishness and wide-eyed
wonder. Her love life since had been a bit uneven but, much as I was
happy to step up to the plate, her staunch Catholicism proved an
unexpected obstacle. I am unburdened by any religious guilt in that
regard, but luckily for me, I am not a Catholic.

We beetled over to the car and headed back to the city. It had
been a diverting morning on multiple levels, but my tummy was
rumbling. Lillian drove downtown. We arrived outside what, superficially at least, bore more than a passing resemblance to a hole in
the wall. We sneaked around the busy counter, turned left and were
guided into the restaurant. It was crowded, a roiling mass of people eating, drinking, hollering, shouting, standing up, sitting down,
banging their fists, shielding their eyes. I never realised Sunday lunch
could be such an emotionally charged affair until I looked up and saw
a television perched overhead. There was only one thing to say. Good
golly, Miss Molly! It was showing an international football friendly
between Mexico and the US. I silently wept tears of joy.

The Mexicans, the away team, were a goal up when we got there,
two up by the time we ordered and proceeded to score five without
reply. Much of our conversation was peppered with spasmodic pas-
sages of song as the mood swayed. It was a fairly tight game until the
latter stages, when the Mexicans ran away with it. I had the added
pleasure of watching Carlos Vela of Arsenal FC, true purveyors of the
beautiful game, strut his stuff and chip a sublime goal of his own.
The food came a pretty close second, however. Lillian took charge
and a series of dishes appeared at regular intervals. There was enough
to feed a family of six, but I rose to the challenge. I dipped in and
out as I intermittently watched the match, nodded supportively at
Lillian's tales of family life chez Fox, admired her pert and comely
form and absorbed the atmosphere. I believe it's called multitask-
ing. Game over, the fiesta spirit subsided somewhat despite sporadic
manifestations of man love as the male of the species were moved to
share the experience with one another, again and again. The Mexicans
so love their football. Bless them all.

We settled the bill and stepped outside. It was now late afternoon. Lillian asked if there was anywhere I would particularly like to

go next. I said that I wanted to check out two districts, Condesa and Roma. They are next door to one another and represented a different side of the city. Slightly raffish and bohemian, they sounded right up my rue. This was the creative hub and promised to give me a real flavour for the capital. Lillian seemed a bit concerned that I would be a little boy lost in a dark and dangerous hood. I reassured her that I was forty-seven and I should be able to cope with any unexpected complications such as losing my compass or speaking to strangers. I had plenty of form in that regard.

Meanderings in Marrakech

Indeed, the previous year I found myself deep in the medina in Marrakech, lost beyond compare, having shaken off a gaggle of kids who variously offered a private tour of the souk, a personal introduction to their favourite street trader and all manner of earthly delights. Step forward, Mr Bobble Hat. The weather was cold, so I wore my hat, emblazoned with the Arsenal crest. Football is a global language and the mere sight of my sartorial splendour caused a veritable babble of tongues. Although I was in Morocco, their sense of African identity caused them to wax lyrical about Emmanuel Adebayor, the rangy, mercurial centre forward from Togo, who led the line for Arsenal. It was a fine example to me of the unifying force of football and sport more generally. Eventually, still accompanied by my persistent admirers, I wound up in a bar watching a competitive if unorthodox game of table football. Plenty of fancy footwork was on display, explosive finishing, showboating and profuse thanks to Allah. I was tempted to put a few dirham down as a mark of intent but mused over a hint that my powers at the table might be in gentle decline.

Some twenty years prior, I had purchased a table football with five friends. We all chipped in £50 towards its cost, but it resided in my flat, as I had a bit more space. As a result, whenever we gathered to play, I was present and correct and my game, sound since childhood, improved immeasurably. Once I was married, thanks to the good grace and culinary skills of my ex-wife, I even hosted day-long mini-tournaments but then kids intervened, one, two, three in pretty short order and my dedication to the table temporarily waned. However, as soon as they were able to walk, talk and go to the toilet by themselves, I sensed a new day was dawning. Once they could turn the handles and peer over the top, I was back in business. We played singles and doubles, different combinations and with a slightly unconventional scoring system. Points were also awarded for sportsmanship, complimenting the opposition, not going into meltdown when your partner conceded yet another goal, looking pretty, getting me a drink—all lessons in life. My daughters more than held their own, but my son really took to it and, in due course, he started giving me a serious run for my money.

Rube proved to have quick hands and a competitive spirit. By the time he was nine or ten, I played him as I would with my friends. It was the first to ten; I would give him a 7–0 start and, without unduly extending myself, beat him, but he grew progressively more determined, wherein it grieved him deeply when apparent victory was snatched away at the last. Suddenly, I was giving him a four-goal advantage, and then we were going head-to-head. By the time he was a teenager, he was pushing me hard and I sensed, quivering at the margins, a changing of the guard. There were a few near misses when the intensity of his game, the flick of his wrist, my beads of perspiration, threatened to tilt the balance his way. And then it happened. He won. He beat me fair and square. I continued to hold the upper hand for a year or two more, but then a perceptible shift in power ensued. He was too lithe, too strong, too focused. "There goes the glory of youth," I said through gritted teeth. And then there was the banter, the goading, the physical contact, the running commentary—nothing malicious, but a challenge laid down nonetheless.

We have had some epic encounters, whether best of five, best of three or a one-off. There are only three explicit rules. No spinning at any time, unless you are under five and can't quite see the action; goals may be scored directly from kick-off should one get a lucky ricochet; and shots struck with such venom they bounce back into play from the goal do not count. It's the kind of game where a supposedly unassailable lead can become vulnerable and then magically or tragically disappear. It's the kind of game where I am losing 6–1 and wondering where the warm-up went. It's the kind of game where, if I make a fast start and match his aggression and power, I can remind Rube that form is temporary but class is permanent. Admittedly, I don't remind him of that too often these days, but standing at that bar, whimsically reflecting upon my past exploits, I thought I could perhaps handle this, can still punch my weight, have a bit of a crowd behind me before realising my erstwhile companions had got bored and sought easier prey.

Relieved to finally be on my own, I stepped outside. I was no longer lost, not even hopelessly lost—no, now I was hopelessly, hopelessly lost. The street was quietly bubbling, although tinged with that invisible frisson of menace that often accompanies the unknown. Who or what might appear next? I adjusted my bobble hat and surveyed the scene. Salvation of a kind appeared opposite the bar where a group of four or five men, loitering without much intent, caught my eye. One of them, a little more forward than the rest, spotted a copy of the *Herald Tribune* under my arm, assumed I was an American and started to engage me in conversation. Abdul spoke surprisingly good English for a local guy just hanging around the medina but, as he would reveal to me later, that was because he was an English teacher. More interestingly, he and his friends were openly smoking what he referred to as chocolat but my nose told me was hashish. He offered me a toke as we discussed my impressions of Morocco and the perception of his country by the outside world. And then he asked me around to his place.

This required a fairly hasty value judgement on my part. I had no reason to question his integrity or the sincerity of his invitation, though I must confess, deep in the old city, I did give a moment's thought as to whether I might be bundled in, tethered to a post and corn-dogged, my muffled cries drowned by the hubbub of the market. However, I reasoned that, in the event of any struggle, I was much bigger than him and, besides, who was I to cast aspersions on his intentions? I duly followed him home. It was just a couple of minutes away, a modest affair indeed that he shared with his wife and young son, his brother and his wife, and their widowed mother. We sat upstairs in his living room drinking sweetened mint tea brought by his gentle, if ancient, mother, who dutifully placed a special tablecloth under the tray while Abdul proceeded to roll a joint of impressive proportions. We chatted some more about the limitations of the Moroccan educational system that determined that Abdul only worked half days, his dreams for his son and his country, the honour he felt that I had accepted his hospitality. It was very humbling to hear him speak in these terms and I felt rather ashamed that I had ever doubted him.

I hoped to meet his son, no more than six or seven, to give him my Arsenal bobble hat personally, do my bit for international relations, but it transpired that Nabil was at the hammam with his mother. Lucky lad. I don't ever recall being taken by my mother to nestle in layers of womanhood, bathe amidst their fragrance, discern the various contours of the female body, develop secret crushes. Clearly, hammams were in short supply in North London in those days. I trusted that Nabil was taking it all in and enjoying the show; he would be dispatched to the men's room long before the first wisps of puberty emerged. The provision of a hammam is such a practical and enlightened custom, delivering togetherness and solitude, a place of refuge and sanctuary. It purifies mind, body and soul. Moreover, when we are stripped of the veneer of clothing, it becomes a great leveller. You see people for what they really are. I am a big fan of the hammam. I am also rather partial to its cousin, the steam. My first exposure was in Turkey as a young man, and the pleasure has never diminished. Difficult to match the grandeur of the public baths in Budapest or the quintessential style of Sauna Deco in Amsterdam, but I like to keep an open mind.

Prior to my arrival in Morocco, I had wrenched my shoulder, engaging in the rigours of a Pilates session, and no end of massage and physio in London had cleared the problem up. Anyhow, the moment I mentioned my shoulder, Abdul said, "Ah!" He repeated himself for good measure: "Ah! You must come with me tomorrow to my hammam. It is a Berber hammam!" To which I responded, "Ah? . . . Ah?" So it came to pass that Abdul took me to the hammam via his abode, where his mother, with a weary smile, plied me with more mint tea.

Here I came to understand the rules of the game. Abdul showed me a minuscule piece of hashish and revealed that this was all that remained from the brick he possessed the previous day. If I were to give him a few dirham, he would pop out and buy some more. He had an excellent source just around the corner. No sooner had I finished appreciating his sleight of hand than he was back, excitedly telling me that his regular supplier was not around but that he had bumped into another source, a bit more expensive but high quality and then asked if I could cover the difference. Needless to say, I took care of business, and we enjoyed a very smooth smoke with our tea. I suddenly then realised, with a clarity surely induced by my stoned condition, that I had brought no accoutrements for the hammam. Abdul had everything under control. He lent me a freshly laundered towel, robe, pair of shorts and a bar of his special soap for scrubbing. His generosity knew no bounds.

We weaved through a maze of alleys until we arrived at an unmarked building, most remarkable for the fact that it remained intact. Like so much else in the old city of Marrakech, it looked as though it was on the verge of collapse but was propped up by centuries of history, community and religious conviction. There was no sign to indicate its presence, but I could sense the sweat staining the walls. It was dark and dimly lit, but Abdul ushered me in and greeted a couple of fellows sitting on their haunches, drinking tea and smoking hashish. I had consumed quite enough of each for now but, conscious of respecting my new hosts, I modestly obliged on both fronts. Various regulars wandered in and out, salaam here, a nod there, the eyes had it elsewhere. The vibe was good but I had little doubt that I was an object of some curiosity, probably one of the very few Caucasians to ever step inside their hallowed portal. Abdul aside, nobody spoke English. A few men were conversant in French but, overwhelmingly, they spoke in a Berber dialect.

Meantime, one of the men we greeted at the entrance, wiry, taciturn, severe, trailed off down a corridor, and I peered through the gloaming. It was very rudimentary, a bathing facility for the working man, comprising hammams, running pools and areas for discourse, rest and rumination. It was decidedly men only. Abdul told me that there was a similar place just across the street for women. I presumed it was slightly more decorous than the one I was standing in, so basic it did not even have a ubiquitous photo of the king on the wall, a staple of every kind of establishment. I noticed a large luggage rack above. That, Abdul informed me, is where everybody kept their possessions. I realised I was standing in the changing room. There were no lockers, there was no customer service desk and I was certainly going to be hard pressed to get a strawberry and banana smoothie.

Mr Severe drifted back into view, now just wearing a sort of dhoti, and Abdul urged me to get undressed too. I told myself to relax. What could possibly go wrong? All I needed to do was peel off in front of the assembled, slip into the spare shorts and proceed like a lamb down the corridor into the steamy, murky hammam. I had seen an uncommon number of lambs in Marrakech already, feet trussed, carried overhead, cradled in arms, on the back of motorbikes, roofs of

cars, triumphantly borne to their fate. It was near the end of Rama-
dan and, as I was to discover, they were to be ritually slaughtered to
celebrate the Eid. They say timing is everything.

Yet as I passed my clothes to Abdul for safekeeping, I also realised
I was handing my passport, my keys, my cash, my credit cards, my
phone, my life to a man I met only yesterday. I was strangely calm as
I envisioned newspaper headlines of a naked, incoherent British man
found wandering in distress through the casbah. Mr Severe led the
way and we turned into a chamber that, blinking through the thick
vapours, I could see was the hammam. It was almost stiflingly hot and
I noticed out of the corner of my eye a furnace, stoked by burning
coals. This was not quite the sizzle I was expecting.

Mr Severe pointed to the floor. Was there an interesting inscrip-
tion I should be admiring? I smiled hopefully. He did not return the
compliment. He motioned to me to crouch. I looked as though I was
under starter's orders, holding my position, ready to burst out of the
blocks. Instead, he gave me a sharp prod in the small of my back and,
like a collapsible toy, I folded flat on my stomach. He proceeded to
sit astride me, kneading me gently and forcefully by turn, loosening
my muscles. He was up and down, regularly pouring a pail of hot
water over me. I flinched momentarily, but he continued to knead
me, pinching, pummelling, cleansing, two, three, four times until he
considered I was ready for my gommage.

Mr Severe was actually a tayeba, an attendant, there to wash, scrub
and massage me. I was lying face down on the hot, wet floor, vaguely
aware of activity above and around me, my pores opening, my circu-
lation renewed, my impurities expelled. Once I had been sufficiently
softened up, Mr Severe beckoned me with an insistent finger. I was
in no position to argue so followed him into another chamber, rather
more temperate, and, sure enough, I was prostrate again. It seemed
that he would observe the same ritual, but I noticed he was now
equipped with a few tools of his trade, a bit like an itinerant barber,
brushes, creams, lotions, the full package, plus his bucket for good
measure. He doused me with more water and then applied sabon
beldi, a sticky black olive oil soap, all over my body, coating me with
it, back, front, sides. Despite displaying all the finesse of a beached
whale, flapping inelegantly in the shallows, I was starting to feel a
bit more comfortable with the hammam, the heat, the etiquette, my
tayeba.

My confidence was rudely shattered when, after lathering me with soap for the umpteenth time, Mr Severe and I engaged in another game of charades and he enlisted the help of a couple of fellows sitting nearby. I could see one mimicking a breaststroke action while the other cracked his knuckles. The latter was a great bear of a man, eyes shining, teeth glinting, arms outstretched. I wanted to think positively, but perhaps I had seen one film noir too many. I was not sure what may follow, but in an instant, the decision was made for me, and I was prone on the tiles, spreadeagled like a starfish, limbs akimbo, both men enjoined with Mr Severe as they proceeded to chip and chop across my body. It was absolutely wonderful, an exquisite six-hand massage, as they pulled, manipulated and stretched me, individually and collectively. No sooner had my support team got into their stride than they were gone, slipping back into the shadows, but aside from personal ablutions, it was normal practice for bathers to assist one another in the hammam. How very civilised.

Now my tayeba started my *gommage* in earnest. The word has a French derivation and literally means eraser or rubber. It is a process of exfoliation to remove dead skin and is facilitated by the use of a special scrubbing mitten called a *kees*. He worked me over in slow rhythmical movements, then sharply and vigorously, scouring my torso with the kees but always quick to soothe and hydrate me. He continued to crunch and crack but my body by now was so tranquillised, so becalmed, so utterly immersed within this miasma of pleasure that I absorbed the pressure without murmur. Eventually, he signalled me once more to stand up, and I followed him into a third chamber, appreciably cooler. I sat down on the floor against the wall and, after confirming all bodily parts were still intact, I realised the pain in my shoulder had been scattered to the four winds. Mr Severe nodded to me, I nodded to him, and then he was gone.

I drew breath. I was limber, I was glowing, I was quite unrecognisable as myself. After a solid five minutes of staring into space, which I accomplished with consummate ease, I gingerly stood up, opened the door, and there, standing in front of me, was Abdul. He was about to make a presentation to me. Not an honorary membership, in case you were wondering, but my clothes and possessions. He proffered them to me, arms aloft, as if making a gift to the gods. Abdul was rather vertically challenged so, as he recited the entire inventory in his care, all I could see was a talking head. He handed everything over and then he reached into his pocket, fished around for a moment and out popped my mobile. With a beaming smile, he said, "Here is your phone. I kept it especially safe for you." I could have kissed him then and there. I quickly showered, got dressed and found Abdul by the entrance. "Where is the tayeba?" I asked. "I would like to thank and tip him." "No need," said Abdul. "I have taken care of it. How else can I help?" "Well," I say, "I wouldn't mind a shave." "Ah!" he replied. A familiar refrain indeed. "Ah! You must come and see my friend Mohammed, the finest barber in the whole of Marrakech. A Berber barber, no less. And guess what—he is only around the corner." Well, there's a funny thing, I thought to myself.

Off we went and, lo and behold, Mohammed was only around the corner. He seemed slightly around the bend too as, when we approached, I could see he was cutting one man's hair, shaving another, engaging in a very agitated telephone call with a third, while simultaneously conducting an argument with a man in the street. I sat down in the chair, somewhat cautiously, concerned that my request to Abdul for a shave alone has not been lost in translation. I patted my cheeks somewhat theatrically to make my point but Mohammed seemed far too preoccupied to notice. My hair, despite displaying all the consistency of an upturned lavatory brush, is something of a protected species for me, and though it gradually dwindles, I would like it to meet its maker as nature intended. Mohammed stood behind me, and we both exhibited puzzled expressions to each other in the mirror. He was trying to make sense of why the man in the chair was clasping his hands over his head as if nursing a baby pineapple. The man in the chair was trying to make sense of the spectacularly garbled English of the man brandishing the scissors.

We overcame our language barrier and he got down to business. He was quick and efficient and I was soon freshly shaved, powdered and buffed with a squirt of cologne too. How much did I owe? Mohammed glanced at Abdul, as if seeking divine inspiration, and he glanced at me. "Please give whatever you think is right," said Abdul. This was a beautiful answer for which I was wholly unprepared. I gave Mohammed ten dollars and a smile and everyone seemed happy. Abdul took my arm. "And a gift for me?" "Well, of course," I say, and I slipped him a little something. He looked at me rather dolefully. He had his overheads. There was the cost of the hammam and my tayeba, and though he didn't quite put it as such, there was the pleasure of his company and a window into his Berber world. Quite right too. I topped him up, we embraced, I gave him my Arsenal bobble hat as a present for Nabil, and he pointed me in the direction of my riad, which, as luck would have it, was right around another corner.

If I learned only one thing from my various excursions with Abdul, it was a reaffirmation of the fundamental kindness of strangers. But it was underpinned by the reality that the human being is a very social animal and that, in an increasingly wired world, people forget too readily the necessity of physical interaction at work, rest and play. The hammam provides an adhesiveness, as does the shteibel in its own peculiar fashion. It is perhaps why I tend to gravitate towards the communal table in a café to observe, to watch and wonder, to read the newspaper, to gatecrash private conversations and perhaps even to enjoy a spot of lunch. I am there and not there, engaged in a slightly disengaged way. I am OFFLINE.